The Evolution of 20th Century Architecture: A Synoptic Account

Kenneth Frampton

Plate 1 Le Corbusier, Lucio Costa and Oscar Niemeyer, Ministry of Education, Rio de Janeiro, Brazil. 1939.

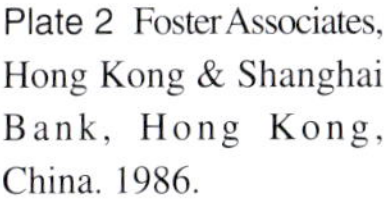

Plate 2 Foster Associates, Hong Kong & Shanghai Bank, Hong Kong, China. 1986.

Plate 3 Renzo Piano, San Nicola Stadium, Bari, Italy. 1987–90. General view.

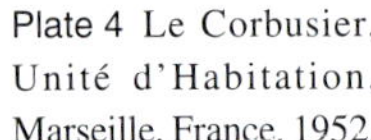

Plate 4 Le Corbusier, Unité d'Habitation, Marseille, France. 1952.

Plate 5 Alvaro Siza, Malagueira Housing, Evora, Portugal, 1960–90. General view.

Plate 6 Thomas Herzog, Halle 26, Hanover Trade Fair, Germany. 1996.

Plate 7 Glen Murcutt, Marika-Alderton House, Arnhem Land, Northern Territory, Australia. 1991–94

Plate 8 Tadao Ando, Rokko Housing, Phase 1, Kobe, Japan, 1978–83. View.

Plate 9 Renzo Piano, Jean-Marie Tjibaou Cultural Center, Nouméa, New Caledonia, 1993. View from the sea.

The Evolution of 20th Century Architecture: A Synoptic Account

Kenneth Frampton

SpringerWienNewYork

China Architecture & Building Press

The Evolution of 20th Century Architecture:
A Synoptic Account

Kenneth Frampton, Columbia University

Printed in China

SpringerWienNewYork is a part of Springer Science+Business Media
springer.com

Editors-in-Charge: Wang Boyang Zhang Huizhen Dong Suhua

Printing: everbest printing

Cover Design: Deb Wood, New York, USA

Layout: Feng Yizheng

Copy Editing: Susan Siegle

Printed on acid-free and chlorine-free bleached paper

SPIN: 11611035

Library of Congress Control Number: 2006934287

With 169 Figures

ISBN 978-3-211-31195-0 SpringerWienNewYork

Contents

Introduction

In the limited space that I have at my disposal, it is obviously impossible to give a truly global history of the evolution of twentieth century architecture. Instead I have attempted to trace different ideological trajectories as these have crossed and re-crossed each other in the course of the century. Hence, I have tried to compile a genealogy rather than a history, and for this reason it is an account which has a markedly fragmentary character due in large measure to what one can only call conceptual fluctuations; that is to say the way in which certain ideas rise to the surface at a given moment, are elaborated and after a while abandoned, only to re-emerge later in a different form. Because of this waxing and waning of these ideas over time, this account will often depart from a strict chronological sequence. To this end, the material is treated under four different headings; *Part 1: Avant-Garde and Continuity, 1887–1986, Part 2: The Vicissitudes of the Organic, 1910–1998, Part 3: Universal Civilization and National Cultures, 1935–1998 and Part 4: Production, Place and Reality, 1927–1990.* The aim of each section is to trace the evolution of different paradigms and to show how a particular theme or cultural trope manifests itself in various ways under different historical circumstances.

The first of these sections deals with the antagonism between avant-gardism and traditional culture as this was to inform many of the initial phases of the modern movement, particularly up to the outbreak of the Second World War in 1939 and again with some uncertainty in the aftermath that followed in 1945. The second section treats with the concept of the *organic*, seen as a generic third term between avant-gardism and tradition, one that seems to have been posited as a strategic alternative to either classical or vernacular culture. The third section traces what we may identify as the diaspora of the modern movement as it is disseminates all over the world, first in the European and North American periphery and then in Latin America, Asia and Japan. In this process it transforms itself as it comes into contact with different societies and climates and with the demands imposed by diverse representational and instrumental needs. The fourth and final section treats with the tension between place and technology. That is to say on the one hand with the need to create and maintain the character of a given place as a "space of human appearance" in the face of an ever expanding technological capability which architects must master in some degree in order to maintain their control over the means of building production.

The third term in the title of the fourth part alludes to the way in which the environment as a whole comes to be realized within the historical moment and the way in which the scope of the architectural intervention is necessarily limited by circumstances. In this regard, one recalls Alvaro Siza's ironically ambiguous aphorism, "architects don't invent anything, they transform reality". The apodictic character of this assertion recognizes that the real is always in some sense already given and that the most that one can do is to modify its substance and form across time in a sensitive manner.

Such a synoptic account cannot in any sense be regarded as comprehensive. It is by definition selective and even, one would have to concede, somewhat polemical. Thus there are innumerable gaps and omissions both within and without the four overlapping trajectories. It should go without saying that an untold number of talented architects do not appear in this account, not because their contribution is not of value but rather because they seem not to have played a key role in relation to the ideological foci outlined above. At its best, this essay can be nothing more than a subjective overview of the diverse evolution of architectural culture across the century. In relation to the broadly regional focus of each particular volume of the anthology, it is hoped that this gloss will be read as a kind of counterpoint, highlighting certain moments, here and there, when a particular architect, building, concept or event makes a salient, if passing, contribution to the apocalyptic continuity of our time.

Part 1:

Avant-Garde and Continuity 1887–1986

... Wherever urban culture blossoms and bears fruits, *Gesellschaft* appears as its indispensable organ. The rural people know little of it. On the other hand, all praise of rural life has pointed out that the *Gemeinschaft* among people is stronger there and more alive; it is the lasting and genuine form of living together. In contrast to *Gemeinschaft*, *Gesellschaft* is transitory and superficial. Accordingly, *Gemeinschaft* should be understood as a living organism, *Gesellschaft* as a mechanical aggregate and artifact.
Ferdinand Tönnies, *Community and Society* [1]

A pastoral view denies the contradictions, dissonances, and tensions that are specific to the modern and sees modernity as a concerted struggle for progress, uniting workers, industrialists, and artists around a common goal. In a view of this sort, the bourgeois modernity of capitalist civilization and the aesthetic modernity of modernist culture are given a common denominator while the underlying conflicts and discrepancies are ignored. Politics, economics, and culture are all united under the banner of progress. Progress is seen as harmonious and continuous, as though it developed to the advantage of everyone and without any significant interruptions. Typical of this view is Le Corbusier's: "A great epoch has begun. There exists a new spirit. There exists a mass of work conceived in the new spirit; it is to be met with particularly in industrial production ... Our own epoch is determining, day by day, its own style." The counterpastoral view is exactly the opposite; it is based on the idea that there is a fundamental discrepancy between economic and cultural modernity, and that neither can be achieved without conflicts and moments of fissure. A counterpastoral view regards modernity as characterized by irreconcilable fissures and insoluble contradictions, by divisions and fragmentation, by the collapse of an integrated experience of life, and by the irreversible emergence of autonomy in various domains that are incapable of regaining their common foundation. Typical, for instance, is the conviction that art is by definition anti-establishment and that enmity between established social interests and avant-garde artists is unavoidable ...
Hilde Heynen, *Architecture and Modernity,* 1999 [2]

1.1 Gemeinschaft versus Gesellschaft 1887–1903

Although the British were among the first to respond to the cultural crisis induced by industrialization, it will fall to German intellectuals to articulate the socio-cultural consequences of this new condition. A key figure in this regard was Ferdinand Tönnies, whose book *Gemeinschaft und Gesellschaft* of 1887 distinguished between the rooted *culture* of agrarian society and the uprooted *civilization* of the industrial city. Barely a decade later the Belgian socialist writer Emile Verhaeren will condemn the burgeoning cities of the industrialized world for having become ominously tentacular. Thus, just as the original medieval foundations expanded well beyond their natural boundaries into the countryside, so the nineteenth century city suffered an exponential growth in its urban population. Manchester's population expanded eightfold in the course of the century to end with a population of 600,000 at the turn of the century, while over the same period, London increased from 1 to 6 1/2 million. The émigré city of New York grew at an even greater rate, passing from 33,000 in 1800 to 3 1/2 million by the end of the century. In central Europe, Berlin, the industrial city *par excellence*, would grow from 180,000 in 1800 to 2 million by the beginning of the twentieth century.

The middle-class reaction to this imploding population was to escape via the convenience of rail transit into the still accessible semi-rural surroundings of the expanding metropolis. Subject to this pressure, the dormitory suburb came into being, served in the case of London's semi-rural surroundings by the Arts and Crafts architect Charles Francis Annesley Voysey, who was to be one of the most talented designers to create an appropriate image for the accommodation of this new-found commuter population. Voysey's stuccoed, whitewashed suburban houses, with their banded fenestration and stone window surrounds, their leaded lights, battered chimney shafts and slate roofs, evoked in a subtle way the lost *Gemeinschaft* character of the yeoman farmhouse. This manner, mixed with the equally picturesque Queen Anne style invented by Richard Norman Shaw around 1870, becomes the *lingua franca* of the British Garden City movement that was founded in 1898 by Ebenezer Howard, through his tract *Tomorrow: A Peaceful Path to Real Reform*. This was to be followed by the establishment of the garden city of Letchworth, laid out to the picturesque designs of Raymond Unwin and Barry Parker in 1903 (Fig. 1). Realizing that one could not return to the *Gemeinschaft* of the pre-industrial era, Howard opted for a compromise combining the benefits of both urban and rural life. This soon became the new paradigm of the satellite city surrounded by a green belt ostensibly designed to restrict further tentacular growth. From this general reflex, there not only followed the proliferation of suburbia throughout the world, but also, half-a-century later, the establishment of the British Ministry of Town and Country Planning that accompanied the New Towns Act of 1946. Endorsing Howard's garden city ideology as the official policy of its post-war socialist government, the British government entered upon a program of ex-urban town building that would be the core of its welfare state policy from 1946 to 1975.

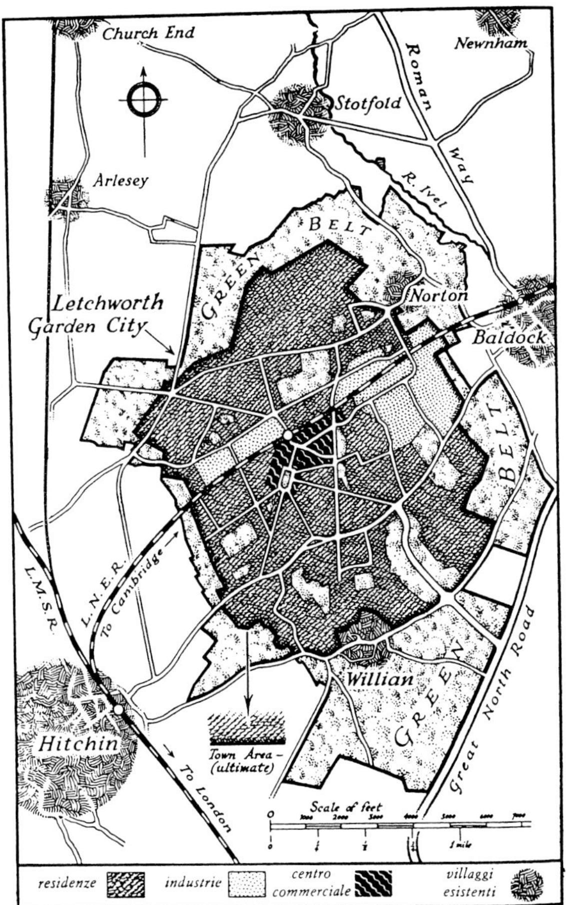

Fig. 1 Raymond Unwin and Barry Parker, Letchworth Garden City Plan. 1903.

1.2 Spoken Into the Void, 1898–1910

Repudiating the self-conscious aestheticism of the *avant-garde*, the Viennese architect Adolf Loos dealt a devastating blow to the prestige of the Austrian *Jugendstil* when he returned from his three-year stay in America to announce to all concerned that there was nothing more important for the maintenance of civilization than the provision of an adequate water supply, as set forth in his essay of 1898, "The Plumbers". In this way, Loos was able to disregard the niceties of the current aesthetic debate by insisting that technological modernization had a life of its own. He cut across the division between *Gesellschaft* and *Gemeinschaft*, by demonstrating how both town and country were exposed to the play of technology to an equal degree and how this was essential to their continued prosperity. Despite his playful irony, Loos saw with a certain melancholia that he shared with his kinsman, the philosopher Ludwig Wittgenstein, that what is "torn must remain torn", which for him meant that neither architecture nor ornament were possible any longer, at least not in the pre-industrial sense of these terms. For Loos, neither the vernacular nor the classical were truly available to the deracinated, metropolitan secular society of his time, as he never ceased to remind his readers in one polemical tract after another. His famous essay, "Ornament and Crime" of 1908, is to be seen in this light, as is the equally challenging essay that came out two years later under the heading, "Architecture". Where the first reminded his compatriots that men live at the same time in different periods of history, particularly for the passage in which he distinguishes between his own self-effacing taste and the ornamental eroticism of his shoemaker, the second began by asserting that culture in the deepest sense of the term cannot be self-consciously cultivated or experienced by the uprooted metropolitan figure, no matter how educated he or she may be. As he would put it, "I call culture that balance between inner and outer man which alone can guarantee reasonable thought and action." To this end his 1910 essay begins with the words:

> May I lead you to the shores of a mountain lake? The sky is blue, the water green and everything is profoundly peaceful. Mountains and clouds are reflected in the lake, and so are houses, farm-yards, court-yards and chapels. They do not seem manmade, but more like the product of God's workshop, like the mountains and trees, the clouds and blue sky. And everything breathes beauty and tranquility.
>
> Ah, what is that? A false note in this harmony. Like an unwelcome scream. In the centre, beneath the peasants' homes which were created not by them, but by God, stands a villa. Is it the product of a good or a bad architect? I do not know. I only know that peace, tranquility, and beauty are no more ... The peasant does not do this. Nor the engineer who builds a railway to the shores of the lake or draws deep furrows through the clear mirror-like surface, with his ship ...
>
> And I ask yet again: Why does the architect both good or bad violate the lake? Like almost every town dweller, the architect possesses no culture. He does not have the security of the peasant to whom this culture is innate. The town dweller is an upstart.[3]

Here technology is a benevolent third term that cannot be reduced to either the classical or the vernacular. It is, as it were, an indifferent transforming instrument of which architecture, like all human endeavors must now take cognizance. Without romanticizing technology in the manner of the Futurists, Loos valued it for its self-effacing instrumentality. Thus his Goldman and Salatsch store (the so-called Looshaus), erected opposite the Hofburg in the heart of Vienna in 1910 (Fig. 2), conceals the long-span reinforced concrete frame by which it is sustained, while making disjunctively ironic allusions to the "lost culture" out of which its form is ostensibly compounded; not only in the four marble, non-load bearing Tuscan columns that represent the civic deportment of the main entrance, but also in the ten, full-height, recessed bay windows, situated on the first floor to either side of the portico; an anti-classical form of gridded fenestration symbolic of the time-honored craft of tailoring which was pursued within.

Fig. 2 Adolf Loos, Goldman & Salatsch Store, Michaelerplatz, Vienna, Austria. 1910.

Later in his 1910 essay, Loos will stand the entire cultural enterprise on its head by showing the extent to which elite culture is of necessity removed from everyday life, so that neither subversive art nor self-conscious architecture can hope to become integrated with society as a whole. To this end there follows the famous passage:

> A house should appeal to everybody, as distinct from works of art which do not have to appeal to anyone. The work of art is the artist's private affair. A house it not. The work of art is put into the world without there being a function for it. A house supplies a need. The work of art is answerable to no one. The work of art aims at shattering man's comfortable complacency. A house must serve one's comfort. The work of art is revolutionary, the house conservative. The work of art points man in the direction of new paths and thinks to the future. The house thinks of the present. Man loves everything that serves his comfort. He hates everything that wants to tear him away from his secure and safe position and is burdensome. And so he loves the house and hates art.[4]

By virtue of this didactic critique, Loos comes close to anticipating the position of the Neue Sachlichkeit architect Hannes Meyer vis-à-vis the priority to be given to *building* rather than *architecture*. At the same time, as in the Looshaus, he fails to endorse the Futurist-cum-Constructivist enthusiasm for the transparency of technology as an end in itself. Thus by implication, he comes to distinguish between four inter-related terms, on the one hand between art and building, on the other between *classic and vernacular* culture, as categories that cut across the emerging opposition between avant-gardism and tradition.

1.3 Italian Futurism 1909–1913

Against the ameliorative Anglo-Saxon response to the socio-cultural crisis induced by the great city, the Italian poet and cultural polemicist Fillipo Tomasso Marinetti proclaimed the unprecedented liberative virtue of the modern metropolis. This positive appraisal of the city as a vast anarchic machine burst upon the world stage with his *Founding and Manifesto of Futurism*, published in the French bourgeois newspaper *Le Figaro* in 1909. Having remained half-poised in the background through the second half of the 19th century, the cultural-cum-political avant-garde finally came into its technocratic own with the emergence of Italian Futurism, as we may judge from the following passage in the initial manifesto:

> We will sing of the stirring of great crowds-workers, pleasure-seekers, rioters-and the confused sea of colour and sound as revolution sweeps through a modern metropolis. We will sing the midnight fervour of arsenals and shipyards blazing with electric moons; insatiable stations swallowing the smoking serpents of their trains; factories hung from

> the clouds by the twisted threads of their smoke; bridges flashing like knives in the sun, giant gymnasts that leap over rivers; adventurous steamers that scent the horizon; deep-chested locomotives that paw the ground with their wheels, like stallions harnessed with steel tubing; the easy flight of aeroplanes their propellers beating the wind like banners, with a sound like the applause of a mighty crowd.[5]

Apart from its debt to the *aeroposeia* of the Italian nationalist Gabriele D'Annunzio, this passage was not only an evocation of the political potential of the masses but also an appraisal of the transformation of modern life through industrialization, together with the extension of the rail infrastructure across every geophysical barrier, the advent of aviation and the growing availability of electrical power. In the face of nostalgically romantic, neo-classical taste, Futurism extolled the virtues of temerity, energy and audacity, while asserting the supreme magnificence of mechanical speed and declaring a racing car to be more beautiful than the Winged Victory of Samothrace.

However, for all its opposition to the romantic fantasies of the Art Nouveau and the Anglo-Saxon Arts and Crafts movement, the form that a Futurist architecture should take was far from clear. In the event, metropolitan form as this had spontaneously evolved in Europe during the first decade of the century would determine the image of the Futurist city as envisioned by Antonio Sant'Elia in his drawings for the Città Nuova, exhibited in Milan in 1914. Thus the superimposed street and transportation systems that appear at the base of his dramatically stepped high-rise apartment buildings were influenced by the metropolitan railways that had been introduced into Paris and Vienna at the turn of the century and by the set-back apartment block that Henri Sauvage built in the rue Vavin, Paris in 1912 (Fig. 3). These are the structural and infrastructural innovations that make up the fabric of the *Città Nuova* as elaborated in the text that accompanied Sant'Elia's exhibition:

> Calculations of the resistance of materials, the use of reinforced concrete and iron, exclude "Architecture" as understood in the Classical or traditional sense. Modern structural materials and our scientific concepts absolutely do not lend themselves to the disciplines of historical styles ... We no longer feel ourselves to be the men of the cathedrals and ancient moot halls, but men of the Grand Hotels, railway stations, giant roads, colossal harbours, covered markets, glittering arcades, reconstruction areas and salutary slum clearances.
>
> We must invent and rebuild *ex novo* our Modern city like an immense and tumultuous shipyard, active, mobile and everywhere dynamic, and the modern building like a gigantic machine. Lifts must no longer hide away like solitary worms in the stairwells, but the stairs-now useless-must be abolished, and the lifts must swarm up the façades like ser-

Fig. 3 Henri Sauvage, Apartments, rue Vavin, Paris, France. 1912.

> pents of glass and iron. The house of cement, iron and glass, without carved or painted ornament, rich only in the inherent beauty of its lines and modeling, extraordinarily brutish in its mechanical simplicity, as big as need dictates, and not merely as zoning rules permit, must rise from the brink of a tumultuous abyss; the street which, itself, will no longer lie like a doormat at the level of the thresholds, but plunge stories deep into the earth, gathering up the traffic of the metropolis connected for necessary transfers to metal cat-walks and high-speed conveyor belts.[6]

Certain inventions were essential preconditions for this mechanical urban vision to come to fruition; among them, the passenger elevator, as this had been installed in New York and Chicago during the last two decades of the nineteenth century, and the perfection of reinforced concrete construction, by the French builder-inventor, François Hennebique in 1896.

Far from restricting itself to architecture, Futurism sought to radicalize every cultural endeavor, particularly during the first phase of its development between 1909 and 1914; thus literature, poetry, painting, sculpture, music, theater, photography, film and clothing successively became the subject of a series of manifestos including even such eccentric themes as Valentine de Saint-Point's *Futurist Manifesto of Lust* or Luigi Russolo's *The Art of Noises*, both dating from 1913. Thus Futurism became the quintessential avant-gardist mode that Italy bequeathed to the world on the eve of the first, industrialized war and it is this that will be enjoined by the European avant-garde after the war when an absolute rupture with tradition will be seen as the essential and inevitable consequence of modernization, first, in the general cultural exuberance that attended the Russian Revolution of 1917 and then in the more restrained and transcendental Dutch Neo-plastic movement that was founded in The Netherlands with the publication of the De Stijl manifesto in 1918.

1.4 Russian Constructivism 1917–1930

By the eve of the First World War, the progressive Russian cultural scene had already given rise to two opposed modes of avant-gardism, on the one hand the painter Kasimir Malevich's dematerialized vision known as Suprematism; on the other the Organization for Proletarian Culture founded by Alexander Malinovsky in 1906. Following the Revolution, this last evolved into the different kinds of *agit-prop* manifestations that sought to forge a new socio-cultural unity from the material and cultural exigencies of socialism; hence the agitational Cubo-Futurist street art of the time and the painted propaganda trains and ships that were equipped to spread the message of the Revolution during the period of War Communism which lasted until 1922. In 1920 Inkhuk (the Institute for Artistic Culture) and the Vkhutemas (Higher Artistic and Technical Workshops) were founded in Moscow as radical schools for training in the fields of applied art and architecture. The Vkhutemas immediately became an arena for intense public debate, above all between Naum Gabo and Antoine Pevsner, who were the authors of the *Realist Manifesto* published in 1920, and Vladimir Tatlin, who along with T. Shapiro, I. Meyerzon, and Pavel Vinogradov, produced a counter-manifesto, *The Work Ahead of Us*, in the same year. In this, with reference to his tower project for the Third International (Fig. 4),Tatlin wrote:

> The investigation of material, volume and construction made it possible for us in 1918, in an artistic form, to begin to combine materials like iron and glass, the materials of modern Classicism, comparable in their severity with the marble of antiquity.

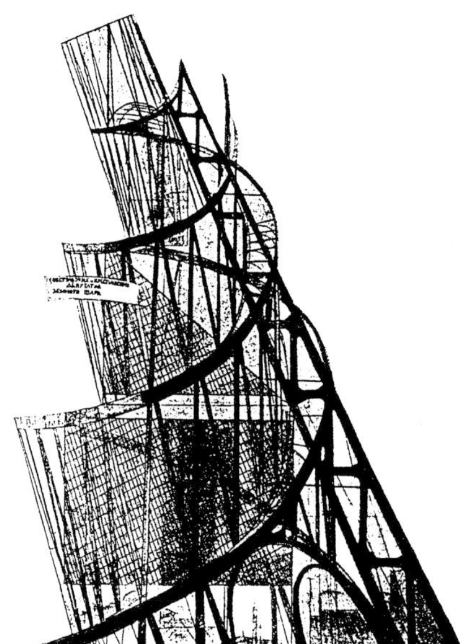

Fig. 4 Vladimir Tatlin, Monument to the Third International. 1920.

> In this way an opportunity emerges of uniting purely artistic forms with utilitarian intentions. An example is the project for a monument to the Third International (exhibited at the Eighth Congress).[7]

Gabo publicly challenged this position and stated in retrospect: "I showed them a photograph of the Eiffel Tower and said, 'That which you think is new has been done already. Either build functional houses and bridges or create pure art or both. Don't confuse one with the other. Such art is not pure constructive art, but merely an imitation of the machine.'" Owing to their claim for the absolute autonomy of art, the Pevsner brothers decided to leave the Soviet Union even though their colleague Malevich elected to devote his energies to establishing his Suprematist School for the New Art. This institution, founded in 1919 under the acronym *UNOVIS*, had a fundamental impact on the artist/designer Eleazar Lissitsky, who was subsequently to play such a seminal role in proselytizing in the cause of international Constructivism, involving his editorship of the short lived tri-lingual magazine, *Vesch Gegenstand Objet*, and his subsequent participation in the Congress of International Progressive Artists at Düsseldorf in May 1922. By this date, most progressive artists in the Soviet Union had abandoned *fine* art in favor of serving the needs of the socialist state as *applied* artists and it is this that created the basis for a momentary fusion between the fields of architecture and art.

The initial consequences of this fusion is evident in the career of the Vesnin brothers who, while they had been committed to Neoclassicism in 1914, were to turn towards Constructivism in 1922, with their steel-framed Palace of Labor proposal that year, festooned with radio aerials. This eminently technological syntax was carried further in their polemical proposal for a totally glazed newspaper building; their diminutive *Pravda* project, furnished with a red flag, a searchlight, a loudspeaker, a digital clock, a rotating billboard and a device for optically enlarging the front page of the paper so as to display it to the street. As Lissitzsky wrote in his *Russia: An Architecture for World Revolution* of 1930:

> All the accessories that the city street sticks onto the building-such as signboards, advertisements, clocks, loudspeakers-even the elevators on the inside, are included as parts of equal value in the overall design and given unity. This is the aesthetic of constructivism.[8]

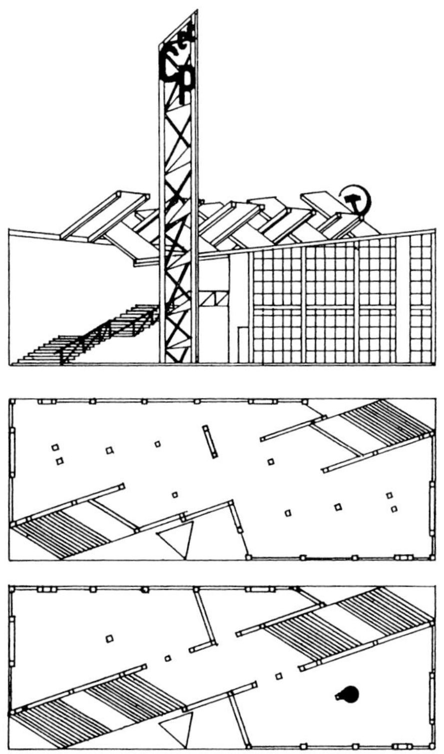

Fig. 5 Konstantin Melnikov, USSR Pavilion, Exposition des Arts Decoratifs, Paris, France. 1925

In the next paragraph, Lissitzky turned his attention to an equally polemical work, namely, Konstantin Melnikov's Soviet Pavilion built for the Exposition des Arts Decoratifs, Paris of 1925 (Fig. 5). After describing the way in which Melnikov's orthogonal volumes had been liberated by the insertion of a diagonal stair, cutting across the plan, he went on to note that

> ... the tower element has been transformed into an open system of pylons. The structure is built honestly in wood, but instead of relying on traditional Russian log construction it employs modern wood construction methods. The whole is transparent. Unbroken colors. Therefore, no false monumentality. A new spirit.[9]

While all the familiar tropes of Constructivism are evident in this work, two different levels of Constructivism emerged at this time, each having distinctly different connotations; on the one

Fig. 6 Grigory and Mikhail Barkhin, Isvestia Building, Moscow, USSR. 1927.

hand, inexpensive, *agit-prop* timber construction such as Melnikov employed, on the other, more technologically and socially ambitious proposals, such as the Soviet Union could hardly afford to realize until the late twenties, as we find this in such buildings as Barkhin brothers *Isvestia* newspaper building, erected in Moscow in 1927 (Fig. 6).

Russian Constructivism was oriented towards evolving a range of building types that could serve as *social condensers*, that is to say, buildings which would be capable of unifying the various constituencies of the new socialist society. Among these types were stadia, swimming pools, theaters, workers' clubs and above all large communal dwellings (Fig. 7). These last frequently assumed radical form, thereby responding to the contemporary debate as to the way in which society should be collectivized, with figures such as the urban sociologist I. Sabsovivich advocating an extremely regimented form of life. Against this the architect Moise Ginzburg, wrote in 1929:

> We can no longer compel the occupants of particular buildings to live collectively, as we have attempted to do in the past, generally with negative results. We must provide for the possibility of a gradual, natural transition to communal utilization in a number of different areas. That is why we have tried to keep each unit isolated from the next, that is why we found it necessary to design the kitchen alcove as a standard element of minimum size that could be removed bodily from the apartment to permit the introduction of canteen catering at any given moment. We considered it absolutely necessary to incorporate certain features that would stimulate the transition to a socially superior mode of life, *stimulate but not dictate.*[10]

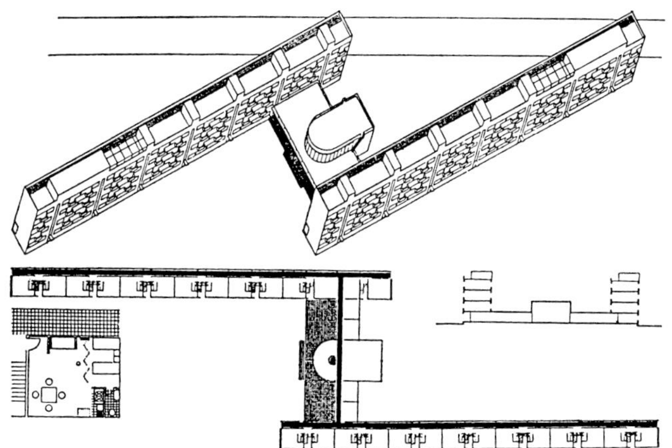

Fig. 7 Moise Ginzburg and the Building Economics Committee of USSR, Dom Kommuna Type A. 1927.

The debate over collectivization was linked to a similar controversy with regard to the future of urban form, with the *urbanists* wishing to densify large towns and *de-urbanists* advocating, after the 1848 *Communist Manifesto*, the dispersal of the existing metropolitan population throughout the countryside. Among the de-urbanists we must acknowledge the linear city theorist, N. A. Milutin, who, in his *Socialist Towns* of 1930, recommended a low-rise, linear city form, running across the landscape in much the same manner as the railway infrastructure or the electrical grid.

1.5 Dutch Neoplasticism 1918–1924

The Dutch Neoplastic movement was a transcendental and extremely idealistic movement by comparison, even though the founding manifesto of 1918 also advocated socio-cultural reform and the need to place a greater emphasis upon the universal rather than the individual. Once again, the creation of the movement was largely the work of artists, namely, Theo van Doesburg,

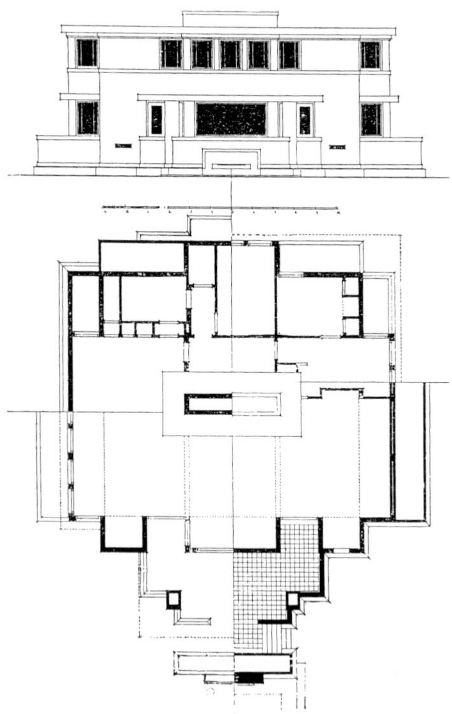

Fig. 8 Robert van't Hoff, House, Huis-ter-Heide, Holland. 1916.

Vilmos Huszár, Piet Mondrian, Georges Vantongerloo and the poet Anthony Kok, even though two architects also added their names to the founding manifesto-Robert van't Hoff and Jan Wils. The first work of consequence to be associated with De Stijl was a house realized by van't Hoff, who had seen Frank Lloyd Wright's work in America before the 1914–18 war. This experience prompted him to build his neo-Wrightian, Huis-ter-Heide on the outskirts of Utrecht in 1916 (Fig. 8). Apart from this pioneering reinforced-concrete dwelling and a number of less elegant Wrightian works by Wils, there was comparatively little architectural activity in the early phases of De Stijl. In fact, the three-dimensional abstract implications of the De Stijl aesthetic were first realized by the cabinet-maker Gerrit Rietveld, in his celebrated Red/Blue chair of 1917, which reinterpreted a traditional chair as a skeleton frame with an articulated seat and back, finished in the canonical De Stijl colors of red, yellow, blue, and black (Fig. 9). This chair, made from inexpensive material, was close to the *agit-prop* works of the Soviet artist/architects Alexi Gan, Alexander Rodchenko

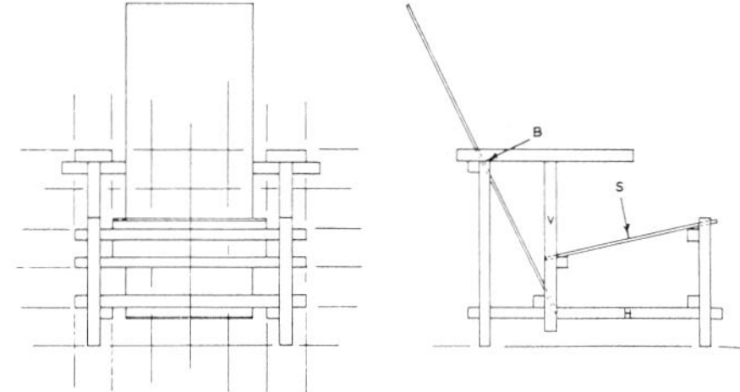

Fig. 9 Gerrit Rietveld, Red/Blue Chair. 1917.

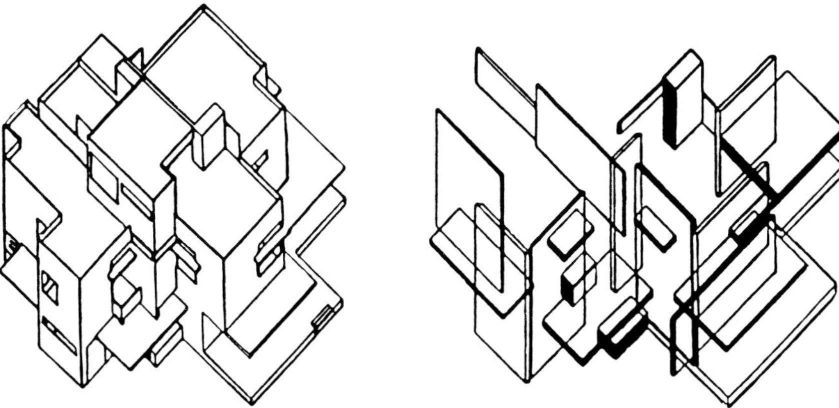

Fig. 10 Theo van Doesburg and Cornelius Van Eesteren, Artist's House as Counter-Composition. 1923.

Fig. 11 Gerrit Rietveld, Schröder-Schräder House, Utrecht, Holland. 1924.

and Konstantin Melnikov. Six years later, Theo Van Doesburg and the young architect Cor Van Eesteren elaborated Rietveld's three-dimensional planar construction into an abstract, pin-wheeling, orthogonal paradigm (their so-called counter-composition) in an exhibition of their joint work, staged in Paris in 1923 (Fig. 10). This asymmetrical, rotating form would be realized, full-size, in the following year with the Schröder-Schräder house built in Utrecht 1924 to the designs of Gerrit Rietveld (Fig. 11).

1.6 The Bauhaus/Germany & USA 1925–1954

The Weimar Bauhaus, foumed in 1919, played a crucial role in the evolution of the European avant-garde not only because it was the pioneering design school of the epoch, rivaling the Soviet Vkhutemas, but also because it was the ideological core around which much of the German modern movement came to be crystallized. We need only pass from its origin in the pre-war seminars given by the pioneer Art Nouveau designer, Henry Van de Velde, to the input of its three successive directors – Walter Gropius, Hannes Meyer and Ludwig Mies van der Rohe – to realize the extent to which, during the first two decades of the century, the main protagonists of German architectural culture were intimately involved with this institution. At the same time the early Bauhaus, as founded by Gropius, was also based on the anarchic, anti-industrial ideology of Bruno Taut as this was advanced after the 1914–18 war, in part through the visionary glass architecture of Paul Scheerbart. However the fact that Gropius had removed himself from the Expressionist fold by the mid-20s is evident from the Bauhaus building that he realized at Dessau in 1925 in collaboration with his partner Adolf Meyer. Like their *Chicago Tribune* design of 1922, the pin-wheeling form of this work testifies to the influence of Neoplasticism, although its cantilevered reinforced concrete skeleton, partly faced in a fully glazed curtain wall, brings this building close to the mainstream of German functionalist architecture of the mid-20s (Fig. 12). Certainly it was more advanced in this regard than Mies van der Rohe's work of comparable date, his concrete-framed, brick-faced Wolf House built at Guben in 1924, even though both works were influenced by Frank Lloyd Wright's Wasmuth Volumes of 1910, particularly as this aesthetic had been filtered through Neoplasticism. With regard to this last, it is significant that while Theo Van Doesburg was never a member of the Bauhaus faculty, he installed himself in a studio close to the Weimar Bauhaus in January 1921 and remained there for nine months with the ostensible aim of subverting the proto-Expressionist ideology then being espoused by Johannes Itten, who was the most charismatic teacher in the Bauhaus at the time.

Hannes Meyer, who succeeded Gropius as director in 1928, was just as removed from Van Doesburg as from Itten. His position lay closer to the hard-line Marxist Constructivism of the *Neue Sachlichkeit*, as is evident from his entry for the League of Nations competition of 1927, designed in association with Hans Wittwer (Fig. 13). Where the formal composition of this work was just as asymmetrical as the Bauhaus, it was based on a modularity that recalled the open-ended assembly of Joseph Paxton's ferro-vitreous Crystal Palace of 1851. Projected as being faced in glass and asbestos cement throughout, Meyer insisted on the absolute transparency of the central circulation tower festooned with the Russian Constructivist iconography, that is an elaborate roof-top radio aerial and an illuminated sky sign. Meyer's appointment as director of the Bauhaus led to the departure of certain members of the faculty, above all Lazlo Moholy-Nagy and Marcel Breuer who, along with Gropius, would migrate to the States, where through their common Bauhaus

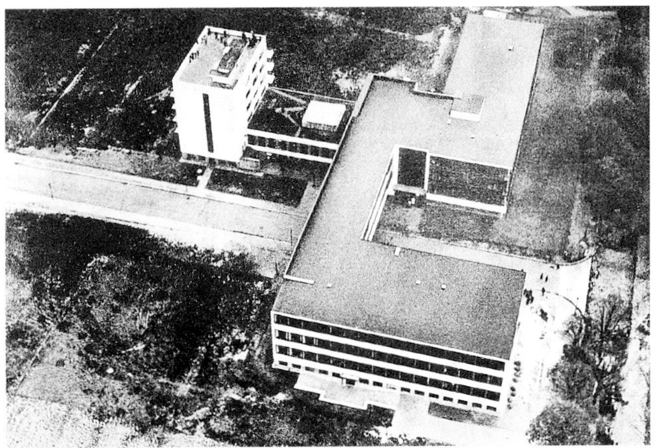

Fig. 12 Walter Gropius, Bauhaus Building, Dessau, Germany. 1925. Aerial view.

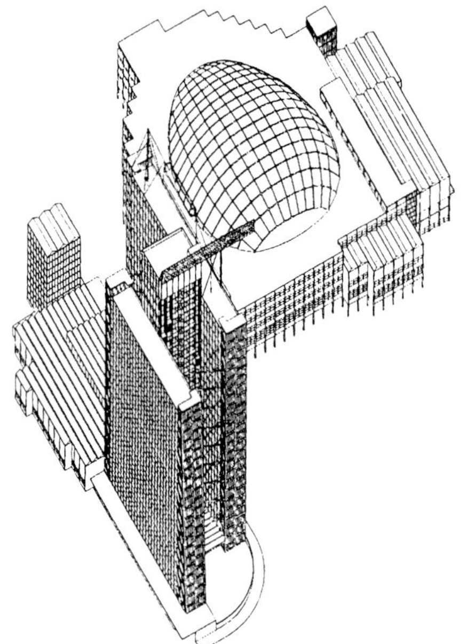

Fig. 13 Hans Meyer and Hans Wittwer, League of Nations project, Geneva. 1927.

formation they would succeed in overcoming the lingering traditionalism of the American Beaux Arts and Art Deco movements. The increasingly reactionary climate of Germany in the late 20s led to Meyer's own resignation from the Bauhaus in 1930, whereupon he also migrated, first to the Soviet Union and thereafter to Mexico in 1932 before repatriating himself to Switzerland in 1941.

Mies van der Rohe succeeded Meyer as director of the Bauhaus at the moment when he had already achieved national acclaim, first with his directorship of the Deutsche Werkbund exhibition, staged at Stuttgart in 1927, and then with the two canonical works that would establish his renown for the rest of his career: the German State Pavilion built for the Barcelona World Exhibition of 1929 and the Tugendhat House realized in Brno in 1930 (Fig.14). Transcending the reductive functionalism that Meyer advocated in his Bauhaus address of 1928, these works were dematerialized space compositions employing large areas of full-height glazing, which, in the case of the Tugendhat House, could be mechanically lowered into the basement, thereby converting the living volume into an open-air belvedere (Fig. 15). This was already Mies' sublime *beinahe nichts*, or "almost nothing", by which he aspired to transcend the techno-scientific rationalism of the 20th century. As he put it in his Bauhaus address of 1930:

Fig. 14 Ludwig Mies van der Rohe, Tugendhat House, Brno, Czechoslovakia. 1930.

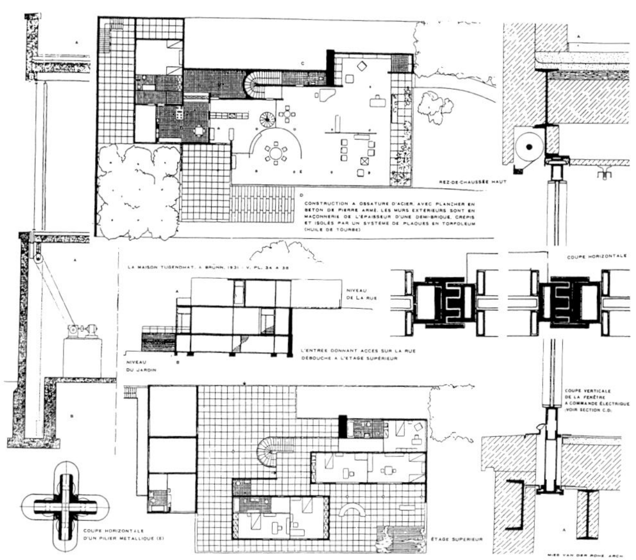

Fig. 15 Ludwig Mies van der Rohe, Tugendhat House, Brno. 1930. Plans, section and details.

Let us not give undue importance to mechanization and standardization.
Let us accept changed economic and social conditions as a fact.
All these take their blind and fateful course.
One thing will be decisive: the way we assert ourselves in the face of circumstances.[11]

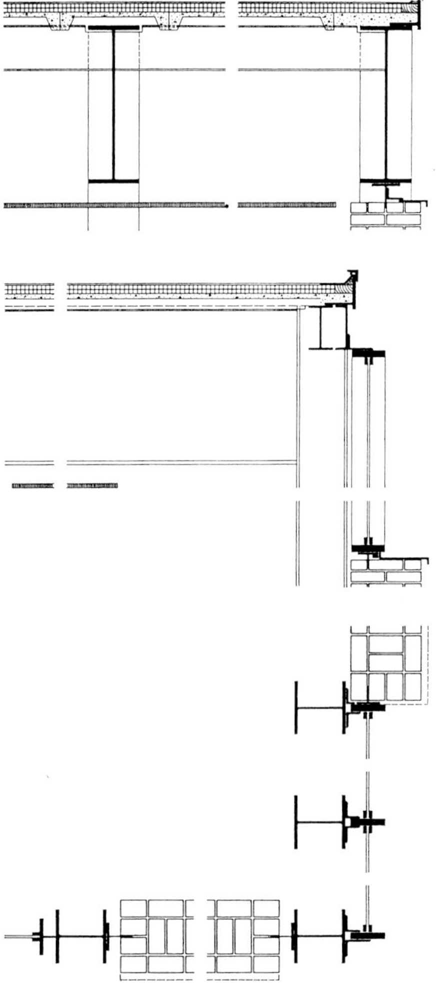

Fig. 16 Ludwig Mies van der Rohe, IIT Library and Administration Building, Chicago, USA. 1942.

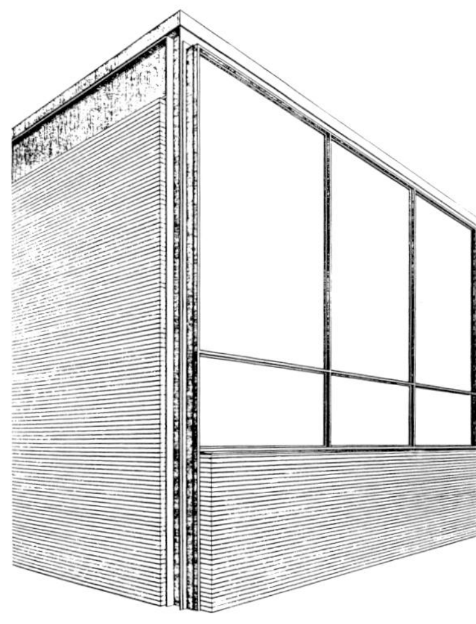

Fig. 17 Ludwig Mies van der Rohe, IIT Library and Administration Building, Chicago, USA. 1942. Construction details.

This allusion to the need for an ethical / spiritual approach to the challenges of modernization would prove to be just as crucial for Mies in political terms, particularly when refusing to compromise with the Nazi regime, he closed the Berlin Bauhaus in July 1933. Thus despite his conservative temperament, Mies maintained a liberal stance, and this enabled him to migrate to the United States in 1937 to assume the directorship of the architecture department at the Illinois Institute of Technology in Chicago. Abandoning the sublime, dematerialized character of his canonical works of the late 20s, Mies now embraced a more pragmatic, steel-framed industrial aesthetic as is evident from his first buildings for the IIT campus, the Minerals and Metals Research Building of 1942 and his unbuilt Library and Administration Building of the same date (Figs. 16 & 17). Mies' characteristically orthogonal, steel-framed skeleton structure filled with large areas of industrial glazing and brickwork afforded a typological model that could be readily assimilated by others, as we may judge from the Neo-Miesian practice of Skidmore, Owings and Merrill during the first half of the 50s; in particular their Heinz Vinegar Plant and the Gunner Mates School, this last being built at the US Great Lakes Naval Training Center in Illinois (Fig. 18). Both of these works anticipated the emergence of High-Tech architecture in Europe in the 1970s.

It is arguable that Miesian typology and methodology played a role similar to that exercised by the Ecole des Beaux Arts at the turn of the century, in that it provided a *modus operandi* that could be readily acquired while still allowing for a certain variation in the evolution of contemporary practice. It is important to note that Gropius or Breuer were not able to influence American architectural production to the same degree as Mies, largely because their adaptation of the pre-war functionalist line to the landscape and vernacular of New England was exclusively domestic, as we find this in Gropius' own white clapboarded, field-stone residence completed at Lincoln, Massachusetts in 1939.

Fig. 18 Skidmore, Owings & Merrill, Gunner Mates School, US Naval Training Center, Great Lakes, Illinois, USA. 1954.

1.7 Rationalism, Purism and Brutalism: France 1923–1965

Despite its wide influence in Europe the abstract centrifugal character of Neoplasticism would render it inimical to further development not only for Rietveld but also for van Doesburg. Thus by the mid-20s the Neoplastic idea had played itself out. Like Frank Lloyd Wright's equally centrifugal Prairie House type of 1901, by which it had been inspired, it was a spatial and compositional format that could only be applied to the program of a free-standing house.

Influenced by Lissitzky's Suprematist-Elementarist relief, as this had been applied to the cubic

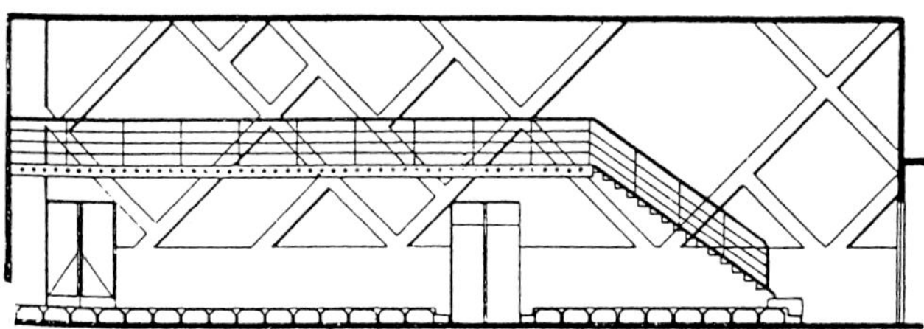

Fig. 19 Theo Van Doesburg, L'Aubette, Strasbourg. 1929. Section through the cinema.

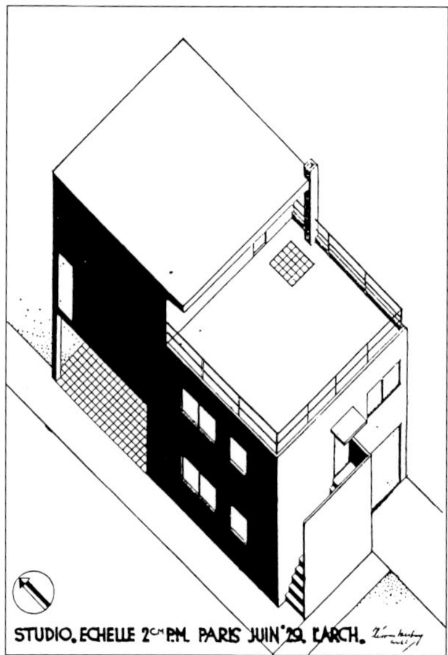

Fig. 20 Theo Van Doesberg. Van Doesberg House, Meudon, near Paris, France. 1929.

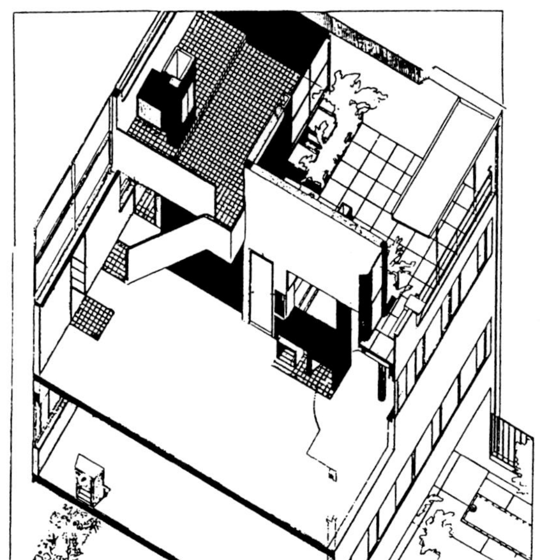

Fig. 21 Le Corbusier, Maison Cook, Bois-de-Boulogne, near Paris, France. 1926.

volume of his *Proun* room created for the Greater Berlin art exhibition of 1923, van Doesburg and van Eesteren became involved with the transformation of orthogonal space through similar relief constructions as these were applied to the interior of the Café L'Aubette, built to their designs at Strasbourg in 1929 (Fig. 19). In that very year van Doesburg designed a house and studio for himself at Meudon, near Paris (Fig. 20), in such a way as to repudiate his "16 points of a Plastic Architecture" proclaimed five years before. In fact the frontalized, cubic form of his Meudon house, structured about a concrete frame and filled in with rendered blockwork and industrial glazing, lay closer to Le Corbusier's Maison Cook of 1926 (Fig. 21) than to the Schröder-Schrader house of 1924. Thus by the end of the 20s the European *art-oriented* architectural avant-garde had already begun to lose its single-minded self-assurance. From now on European modern architecture would be carried forward in a more subtle and mediated way, particularly as this came to be developed in France and Italy during the thirties.

Avant-gardism versus tradition will assume a particularly polemical character in France between the two world wars, as we may judge from Auguste Perret's resignation in 1925 from the editorial board of *L'Architecture Vivante*, a magazine that he had founded barely two years before. The controversy that prompted his resignation stemmed from Jean Badovici's editorial decision to devote the entire 1925 autumn / winter issue of the magazine to Dutch Neoplasticism. As far as

Perret was concerned, this was entirely unacceptable, in as much this mode derived from abstract art and not from the evolving tradition of architecture. At this juncture the antimony was not just between avant-gardism and tradition but more specifically between an abstract aesthetic derived from figurative art and a contemporary tectonic expression grounded in reinforced concrete which Perret conceived as the only viable contemporary technique with which to reinterpret the French neoclassical tradition.

This split between abstract art and tectonic form parallels the slightly different dialectic around which Le Corbusier's *Vers Une Architecture* would be formulated in 1923, that is to say, the dialectic between the Engineer's Aesthetic and Architecture that structures the entire book. Here, while seeing modern technology as affording the basis for a new and more vital architecture, Le Corbusier nonetheless opposes utilitarian instrumentality to the spiritual potential of tectonic form:

> You employ stone, wood and concrete, and with these materials you build houses and palaces; that is construction. Ingenuity is at work.
> But suddenly you touch my heart, you do me good, I am happy and I say: 'This is beautiful.' 'That is architecture. Art enters in.'
> My house is practical. I thank you, as I might thank Railway engineers or the Telephone service. You have not touched my heart.
> But suppose that walls rise towards heaven in such a way that I am moved. I perceive your intentions. Your mood has been gentle, brutal, charming or noble. The stones you have erected tell me so. You fix me to the place and my eyes regard it. They behold something which expresses a thought. A thought which reveals itself without word or sound, but solely by means of shapes which stand in a certain relationship to one another. These shapes are such that they are clearly revealed in light. The relationships between them have not necessarily any reference to what is practical or descriptive. They are a mathematical creation of your mind. They are the language of Architecture. By the use of inert materials and *starting from* conditions more or less utilitarian, you have established certain relationships which have aroused my emotions. This is Architecture.[12]

It was just this Purist dialectic that enabled him to distance himself not only from the *fin de siècle* ideal of the total work of art as this was still latent in the abstract aestheticism of De Stijl, but also from what he saw as the unduly materialistic stance of Constructivism. As he remarked of Constructivism in his book *Une Maison, Un Palais* of 1928, "Where does it begin and end this vague word? It is vague because it contains too much. It admits neither an aesthetic nor a category of production..." Conversely, the Swiss architects Hannes Meyer and Hans Wittwer saw their project for the League of Nations competition as being nothing other than the direct conse-

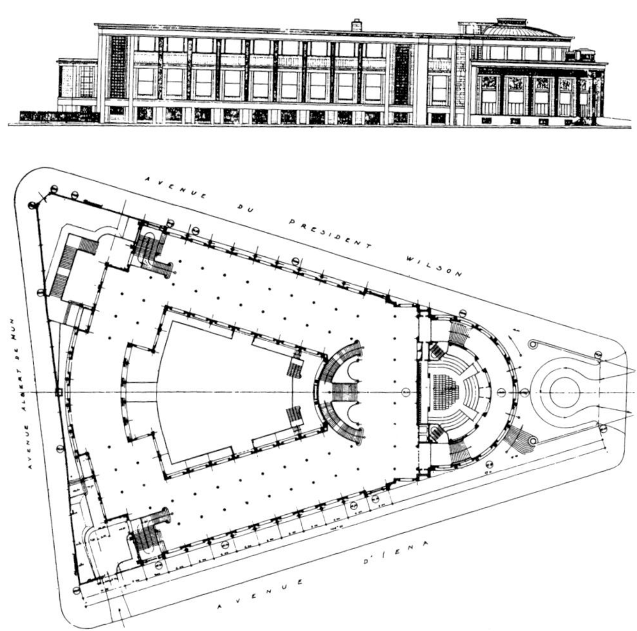

Fig. 22 Auguste Perret, Musée des Travaux Publiques, Paris, France. 1936–54.

quence of techno-scientific production. Hence they conceived of it as *building rather than architecture*, with Meyer writing in 1927:

> Our League of Nations building symbolizes nothing – its size is automatically determined by the dimensions and the conditions of the program ... This building does not seek an artificial link with its park-like setting through the art of landscape gardening. As a deliberately contrived work of man it stands in legitimate contrast to nature. This building is neither beautiful nor ugly. It asks to be evaluated as a structural invention.[13]

In the very same year, in the Autumn / Winter issue of *L'Architecture Vivante*, Le Corbusier set forth his "Five Points of a New Architecture" which, while indirectly acknowledging the latent classicism of the cylindrical free-standing reinforced concrete column, simultaneously proclaimed that the horizontal, sliding window was the typical mechanical element of the house. It is significant that his insistence on sliding steel-framed fenestration would bring him into conflict with his Rationalist master Auguste Perret, who will continue to advocate the traditional, side-hung French window as the essential perspectival frame for the human figure. Hence the vigorous debate that will take

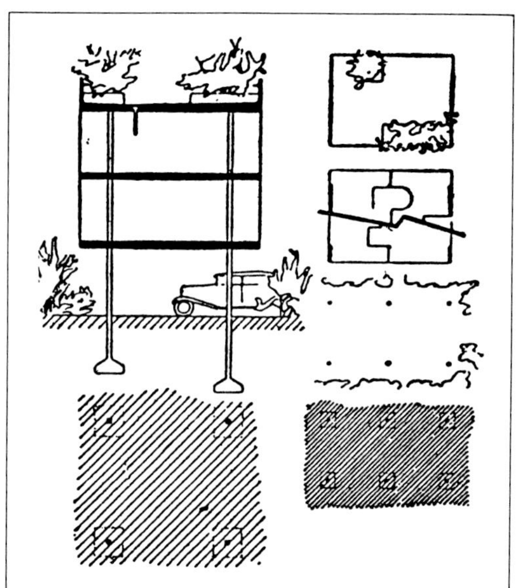

Fig. 23 Le Corbusier, Five Points of a New Architecture. 1926.

place between them as to the relative virtues of the mechanical *fenêtre en longeur* versus the traditional *porte fenêtre*. For Perret this last assured the decorum of the bourgeois interior at an anthropomorphic scale while maintaining the cadence of its space and the gradation of its light.

This schism at the level of detail was symptomatic of the way in which Perret pursued the French, Graeco-Gothic tradition through his expressive reification of the reinforced concrete frame, while Le Corbusier attempted to render the same structural system as a concatenation of free-standing columns. In opposition to Perret's peristylar, monumental vision that attained its apotheosis in his Museum of Public Works, Paris (1936–54) (Fig. 22), Le Corbusier posited the liberated plan and elevation – that is *le plan libre et la façade libre*. These two elements, together with *la fenêtre en longeur, les pilotis et le toit jardin* constituted the aforementioned Five Points of a New (Purist) Architecture (Fig. 23). All in all, as far as avant-gardism in the second half of the 20s is concerned, Le Corbusier situated himself ideologically somewhere between Auguste Perret and Hannes Meyer, with Perret positioned to his political right and Meyer committed to the extreme left.

All of this will be subject to a certain deviation in the next decade as Le Corbusier abandons Purism shortly after the completion of the Villa Savoye in 1929 (Figs. 24 & 25). His subsequent re-

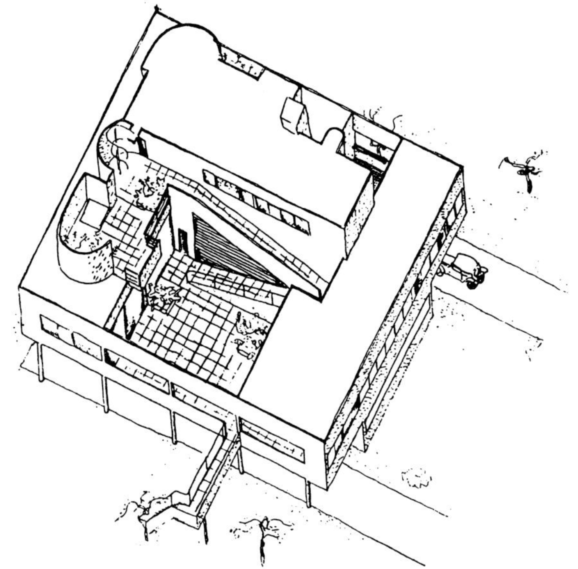

Fig. 24 Le Corbusier, Villa Savoye, Poissy, France. 1929. Axonometric.

Fig. 25 Le Corbusier, Villa Savoye, Poissy, France. 1929. Interior.

interpretation of the "vernacular", which first appeared with his rubble-stone, mono-pitched Errazuris house projected for Chile in 1930, will continue throughout the 30s, culminating in two canonical works, both built in Paris: the so-called Maison Weekend of 1935 (Fig. 26) and the Pavilion des Temps Nouveaux erected for the Paris World Exhibition of 1937 (Fig. 27). Clearly this shift to natural materials and primitive building technique had consequences that went well beyond a mere change in morphology or surface appearance. Above all, it meant abandoning the

Fig. 26 Le Corbusier, Maison Week-End, St Cloud, near Paris, France. 1935.

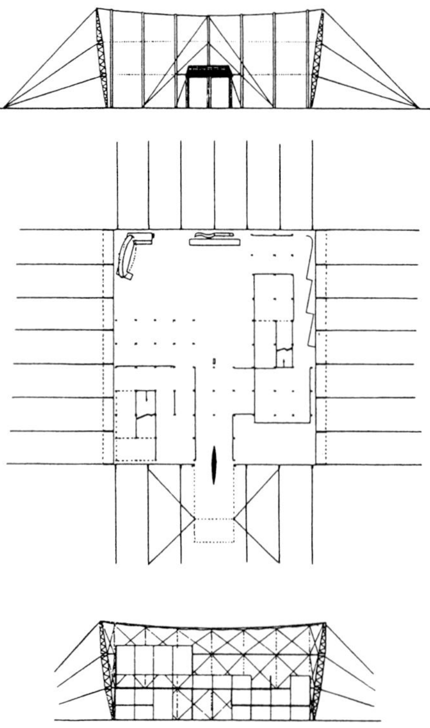

Fig. 27 Le Corbusier, Pavillon des Temps Nouveaux, Paris, France. 1937.

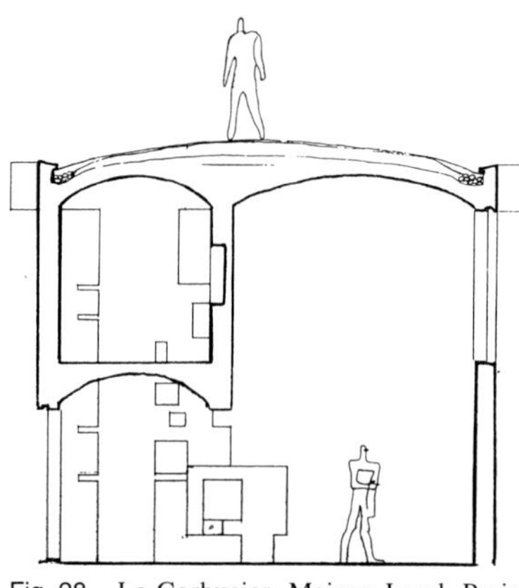

Fig. 28 Le Corbusier, Maison Jaoul, Paris, France. 1955. Section.

crypto-classicism of Purism in favor of an architecture predicated on the expressive force of a single tectonic element, be this a monopitched roof, a barrel-vaulted megaron or a tent, the last being the basic form of the Pavillon des Temps Nouveaux. While the monopitched Errazuris house anticipated the lean-to thatched roofs of Le Corbusier's Maisons Murondin project of 1940, the reinforced concrete shell vault of the Maison Weekend led to his direct use of Catalan vaults in a farm projected for Cherchell, North Africa, in 1942. In fact, Le Corbusier's preoccupation with the megaron type after the Second World War was referential to the Mediterranean vernacular rather than to classicism, as is confirmed by a sequence of works running from his Cherchell project of 1942 to the stepped-terrace housing that he projected for Cap Martin in 1949. This vaulted tectonic culminated in his Sarabhai House, Ahmedabad and in his Maisons Jaoul, Paris (Fig. 28), both dating from 1955, and, by extension, in the canonical, low-rise, high-density, Neo-Corbusian housing scheme known as the Siedlung Halen, built outside Bern, to the designs of Atelier 5 in 1960 (Figs. 29 & 30).

As the British architect James Stirling remarked in the mid-50s, the Maisons Jaoul was an affront to those sensibilities which had been nurtured on the myth that modern architecture should

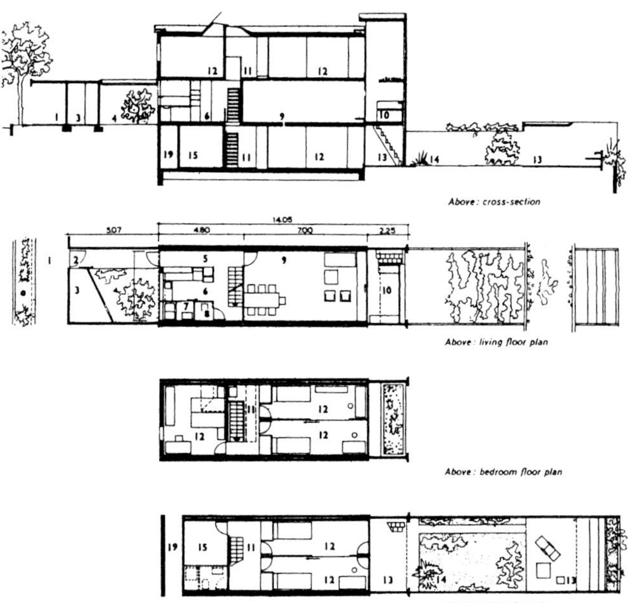

Fig. 29 Atelier 5, Siedlung Halen, Bern, Switzerland. 1960. Plans & sections.

Fig. 30 Atelier 5, Siedlung Halen, Bern, Switzerland. 1960.

manifest itself as smooth, machine-wrought, planar surfaces set within an articulated structural frame. With its narrow vertical windows, Catalan vaulting, exposed load-bearing brick walls and concrete cast straight from rough timber formwork, the Maisons Jaoul presented a tough, tactile reality totally removed from the smooth Purist visions of the 1920s, a pragmatism which was ready to embrace "the contradictions and confusions of suburbia". The syntax of the Maisons Jaoul, the somber aura of which stemmed as much from the unstruck mortar of the brickwork as from the introspective wood-framed windows, was also subtly removed from the equally existential but heroic optimism of Le Corbusier's *Unité d'Habitation* completed in Marseilles in 1952 (Figs. 31 & 32). Returning to the Soviet theme of the collective dwelling, this eighteen-story apartment building was Le Corbusier's last *avant-gardist* gesture in a programmatic sense, even if it was as "brutalistic" in its expression as the Maisons Jaoul; above all for its box-frame concrete structure cast from rough timber formwork. At the same time its vestigial classical feeling arose in larger measure from the proliferation of the golden section ratios throughout by virtue of applying Le Corbusier's proportional system, *Le Modulor*. First developed in 1947, this system will henceforth become an integral part of Le Corbusier's working method, going on to play a crucial role in the remarkable in-situ concrete monuments that grace the last ten years of his life; the Mill Owner's Building, Ahmedabad (1954), the Chapel at Ronchamp (1955), (Fig. 33) the monastery of La Tourette (1960), (Fig. 34) and, last but not least, the capitol complex of Chandigarh in the Punjab, India (Fig. 35); of which the Assembly, Secretariat and High Court will not be completed until 1965, the year of his death.

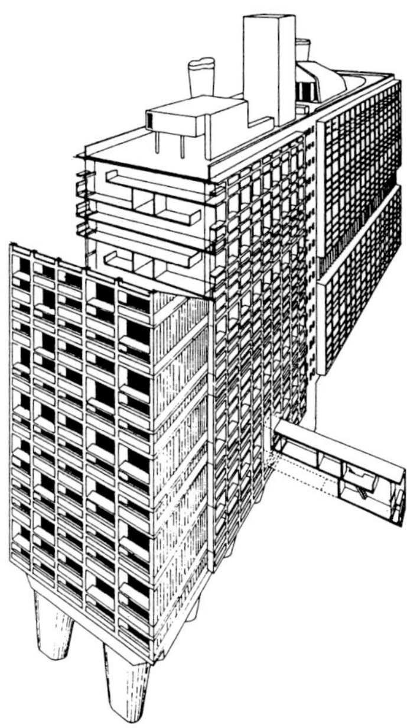

Fig. 31 Le Corbusier, Unité d'Habitation, Marseille, France. 1952. Perspective.

Fig. 32 Le Corbusier, Unité d'Habitation, Marseille, France. 1952.

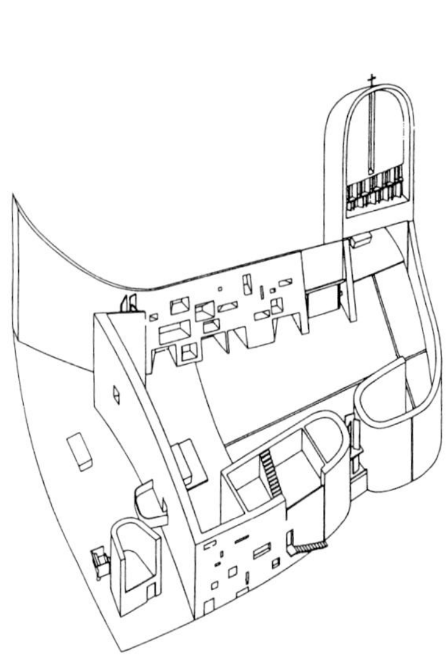

Fig. 33 Le Corbusier, Chapel, Ronchamp, near Belfort, France. 1955. Axonometric.

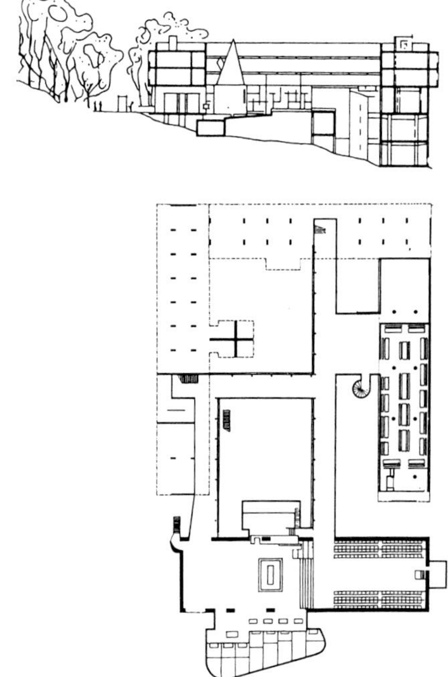

Fig. 34 Le Corbusier, La Tourette Monastery, near Lyons, France. 1957–60. Plan & Section.

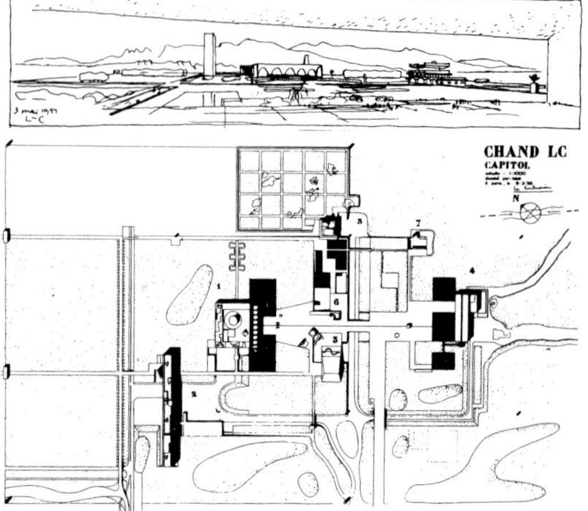

Fig. 35 Le Corbusier, Capitol, Chandigarh, India. 1951–65. Perspective sketch and plan.

1.8 Monumentality and Rationalism: 1923–1980

The years 1923–43 saw a reaction against the pre-1914 Futurist *avant-garde* in Italy. As far as architecture was concerned, this was divided between a rationally mediated modernism and a modernized monumentality. On the one hand there were the young Comasco radicals, the so-called *Gruppo 7* founded in 1926, who sought a synthesis between the rational geometry of classicism and the structural logic of the machine age; on the other, there was the official *stile lictorial* of Marcello Piacentini with its proliferation of loggias, porticoes and blank stone prisms pierced by rectangular windows at regular intervals. Where the former was essentially based upon the structure of the *trabeated frame*, the latter was fundamentally a *wall architecture*, occasionally enlivened by manneristic surface treatments as in the case of Giovanni Muzio's neo-mannerist Ca'Brutta, realized in Milan in 1923. Both positions were affected by the post-war metaphysical artistic movement known as the *Novecento*. Inspired by the work of Giorgio di Chirico, this anti-Futurist manifestation had crystallized in Italy immediately after the 1914–18 war as a movement whose mannered neoclassical historiczing in architecture would be justified

Fig. 36 Edwin Lutyens, Viceroy's Palace, New Delhi, India. 1923–31.

by Muzio in the name of civic form. To this end he wrote in *Dedalo* in 1931:

> A medley of heterogeneous and jarring buildings could never give rise to a new stylistic epoch; concern must be concentrated on complexes of buildings rather than on a single one. It was therefore natural to study the art of building cities, an art hitherto neglected in this country. The best and most original examples of the past were certainly those of classical derivation, and in particular, those of early nineteenth century Milan ... For architecture, as for town planning, a return to classicism seemed necessary, and the same thing occurred in the plastic arts and in literature ...
>
> This could be mistaken for a strange anomaly, the result of a provincial deafness while all Europe was in convulsions and eager for extreme novelty ... but in fact it was an original and deeply-rooted movement. Extremist tendencies had proved inconclusive, since after all links with the past had been done away with ... the doors had been opened to all manner of eccentricities and eroticism. In Italy the cycle was run even faster, and in fact it was here that, after the war, these architects, by reviewing the past, could produce this new classical spirit. Are we not perhaps anticipating a movement whose imminent birth is announced throughout Europe by hesitant but widespread symptoms.[14]

This self-justifying analysis is triply revealing, for while it serves to differentiate the architecture of the *Novecentisi* from that of the emerging Rationalist approach of the *Gruppo 7*, it also correctly characterizes that avant-gardist aporia to which they were both subject, while at the same time

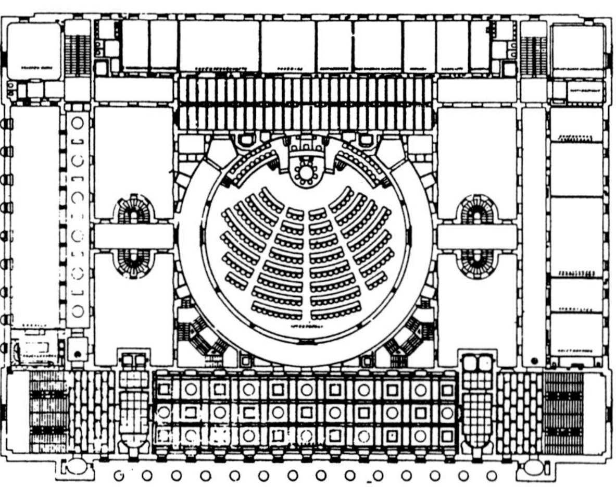

Fig. 37 Johan Sirén, Finnish Parliament, Helsinki, Finland. 1926–31. Plan.

implicitly recognizing the way in which conservative regimes were opting for various kinds of historicizing monumentality, as could be found in the early 30s in works as diverse as Edwin Lutyen's Viceroy's House, New Delhi (1923–31), (Fig. 36) Johan Sirén's Finnish Parliament, Helsinki (1926–31), (Fig. 37) or even Boris Iofan's winning entry for the Palace of the Soviets, Moscow, a

Fig. 38 Boris Iofan, Palace of Soviets, Moscow, USSR. 1931–39. Section.

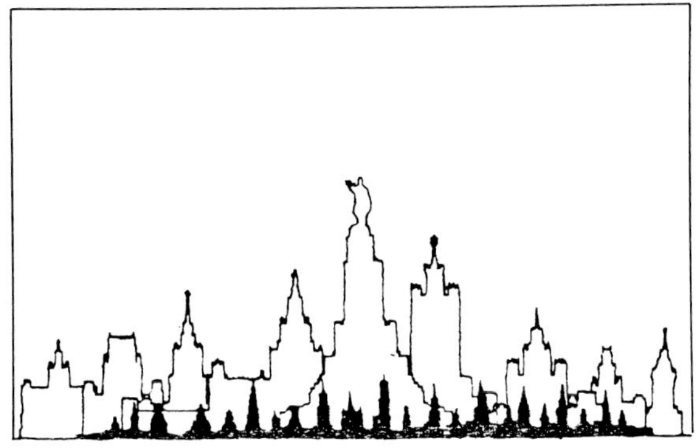

Fig. 39 Boris Iofan, Palace of Soviets, Moscow, USSR. 1931–39. (Outline shows the projected Palace of Soviets rising higher than the other Moscow skyscrapers.)

constructivist-cum-classical hybrid that, subject after 1932 to the dictates of Socialist Realism, became ever more rhetorically monumental over the years, ending in 1934 as a pseudo-classical tower of Babel crowned by a gargantuan statue of Lenin (Figs. 38 & 39).

Nothing could have been further from this than the intellectual monumentality envisaged by the seven members of the *Gruppo 7* – Sebastiano Larco, Guido Frette, Carlo Enrico Rava, Adalberto Libera, Luigi Figini, Gino Pollini and last, but by no means least, Giuseppe Terragni. Their subtle, anti-Futurist but nonetheless progressive position was made abundantly clear in their *Rassegna Italiana* manifesto of 1926 when they wrote:

> The legacy of the avant-garde that preceded us was an artificial impulse – an empty, destructive fury that confused good and bad. The natural right of the youth of today is a desire for *lucidity*, for *wisdom*. We must convince ourselves of it. ... We do not want to break with tradition ... The new architecture, the true architecture, must result from a rigid adherence to logic, to rationality.[15]

In 1932, Terragni produced the main canonical work of the Italian Rationalist movement, the Casa del Fascio in Como. Planned within a perfect square and half as high as its width of 33 meters, the mass of the Casa del Fascio was regulated by a strict geometry (Fig. 40). Within this volume, it not only revealed the logic of its trabeated frame, but also the rational code underlying the modeing of its facades. On every side (except the south-east elevation which stresses the main stair) the fenestration and the external layers of the building are manipulated in such a way as to express the presence of an internal atrium within. Earlier studies for the building reveal that, like other works by Terragni, it was originally planned around an open courtyard. In subsequent stages, this *cortile* became a central double-height meeting hall, top-lit through a glass-concrete roof and surrounded on four sides by galleries, offices and meeting rooms. As in Mies van der Rohe's Barcelona Pavilion of 1929, the monumental status of the entire structure was partially proclaimed by its elevation on a shallow podium. The political purpose of the structure was further expressed through a battery of glass doors that opened onto the piazza at the rear of the cathedral. These, when simultaneously opened by electrical motors, served to unite the atrium with the piazza, thereby not only permitting the unimpeded flow of the political cadre on to the street but also subtly symbolizing Mussolini's rapprochement between the Catholic Church and the Fascist State. Comparable political connotations are evident in the treatment of the main meeting room with its low-relief by Mario Radice and the shrine commemorating martyrs of the Fascist movement. Despite such symbolic features, this work transcended its ideological program in order to obtain abstract spatial effects. To this end the building is treated as though it were an infinite space-field, without any particular orientation such as up or down, left or right, etc. Thus

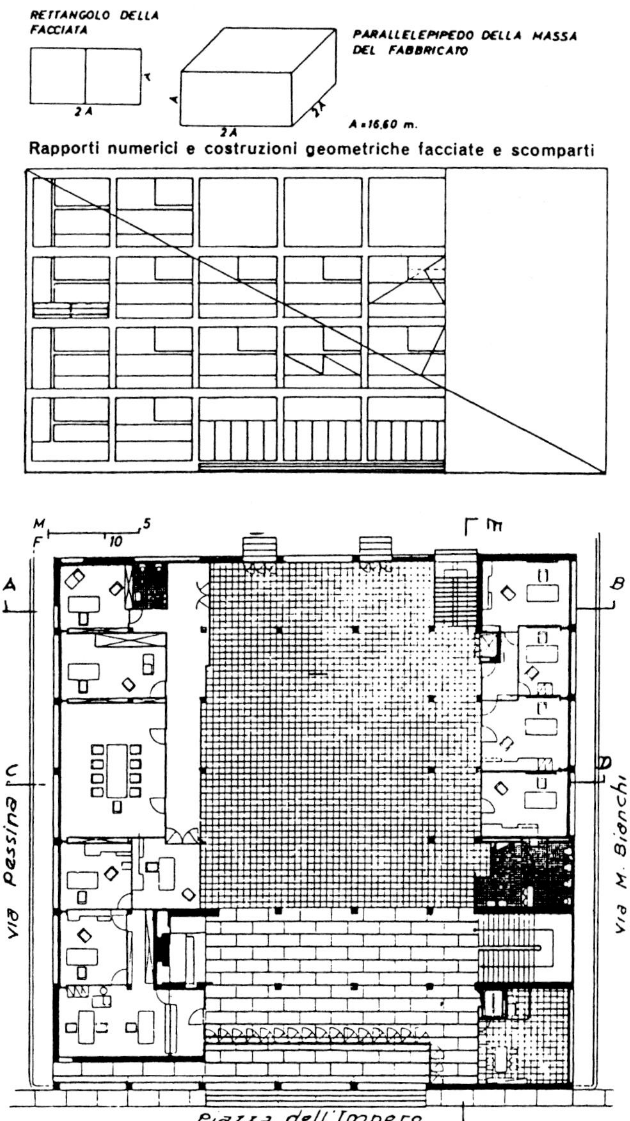

Fig. 40 Giuseppe Terragni, Casa del Fascio, Como, Italy 1932. Elevation, plan & schema.

the piers dividing the entry foyer from the atrium are sheathed in plate glass in such a way as to create the illusion of an infinitely trabeated construction that extends as a ghostly reflection into the polished stone soffit of the ceiling above. At the same time the subtle implantation of the work in an historic urban core, its revetment in Botticino marble and its generous use of glass lenses, serves to create a work which is at once both monumental and machinist.

It is important to note that while they were evidently inspired by Le Corbusier,the Italian Rationalists repudiated his "Five Points of a New Architecture" (1926) which were to exercise such an influence elsewhere. As in the Rationalist work of Perret, but without Perret's classical iconography, the Italian Rationalists insisted upon the authority of the trabeated frame. However they were at times able to temper their neo-Palladianism with a more dynamically functionalist disposition as in Terragni's Sant'Elia School, Como of 1936 (Fig. 41).

After remaining dormant for almost a quarter of a century, Italian Rationalism resurfaced in the early 60s to occupy the center of the post-functionalist debate in Italy, through such polemical

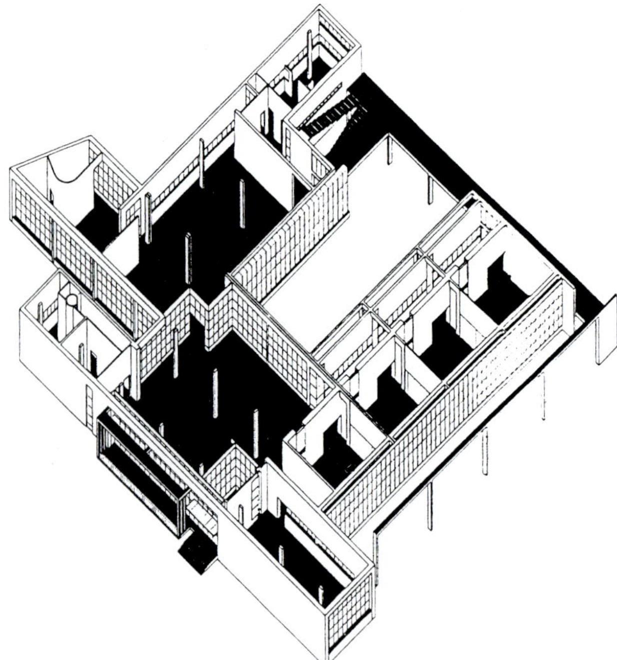

Fig. 41 Giuseppe Terragni, Sant' Elia School, Como, Italy 1936. Axonometric.

texts as Aldo Rossi's *Architecture of the City* (1966) and Giorgio Grassi's *The Logical Construction of Architecture* (1967). In these works it is the typological legacy of Mediterranean classicism that comes to be stressed as the guarantor of monumental continuity within the destabilized fabric of the postmodern city.

Influenced by Emil Kaufmann's theory of architectural autonomy as set forth in his *Von Ledoux bis Le Corbusier* of 1933 and by the conservative socialist thinker Gyorgy Lukács, whose anti-avant gardist *Theory of the Novel* had been first published in German in 1963, Rossi and Grassi sought to return to a rational typological repertoire based on a body of knowledge that was inseparable from the European building tradition. Grassi's point of departure was conceived as an abstract *répétition different* of both classical and vernacular forms. Hence, as the Catalan critic Ignasi de Sola Morales has remarked, "there is no notion in Grassi's work of problem solving, as innovation, or as invention *ex novo*." Like Perret, Grassi adopted an anti-avant gardist stance that he made explicit in his essay, "Avant-Garde and Continuity" of 1980:

> ... as far as the architectural vanguards of the Modern Movement are concerned, they invariably follow in the wake of the figurative arts ... Cubism, Suprematism, Neoplasticism,

Fig. 42 Giorgi Grassi and A. Monestrioli, Students' Dormitory, Chieli, Italy. 1976–86. Perspective and site plan.

> etc., are all forms of investigation born and developed in the realm of the figurative arts, and only as a second thought carried over into architecture as well. It is actually pathetic to see the architects of that "heroic" period, and the best among them, trying with difficulty to accommodate themselves to these "isms"; experimenting in a perplexed manner because of their fascination with the new doctrines, measuring themselves against them, only later to realize their ineffectuality. This is the case of Oud when faced with "De Stijl". It is the same for Mies. Few are immune to it; Loos, Tessenow, Hilberseimer. I emphasize this point because it seems to me today, amid all the confusion, a strong *avant-garde wind* is again blowing our way![16]

Grassi seems to have had the career of Mies van der Rohe in mind when he wrote these words, most particularly with regard to Mies's role in extending the German Neoclassical tradition as one may find this in the architecture of Karl Friedrich Schinkel and Friedrich Weinbrenner and in the 20th century in the equally sober work of Heinrich Tessenow and Ludwig Hilberseimer. This cultural synthesis is particularly evident in Grassi's Student Dormitory completed in Chieti in 1986 after a ten-year building period (Fig. 42). Grassi regarded this range of expression as displaying a normative tradition that could also be found in the anonymous building culture of Southern Europe, such as the repetitive urban fabric of Aigues Mortes or the arcaded rhythmic forms of traditional Tuscan farm complexes. Subject to the influence of the rubble stone and timber house that Le Corbusier built at Mathes in 1935, there is even something of this in Pietro Lingeri's weekend houses built on the island of Comacína in 1938. From this particular example we can see how the Italian Rationalists of the 30s and the Neo-Rationalists of the 60s were to find their common ground not only in the classical tradition for which they both had natural affinity, but also in the vernacular form of pre-industrial society.

Part 2:

The Vicissitudes of the Organic 1910–1998

> The interest which organic architecture (unlike the academic and the stylistic) manifests in man and his life, goes far beyond reproducing physical sensations either directly or indirectly. If for example organic architecture has a feeling of movement and a dynamic quality, this is not achieved through the walls being covered in the Art Nouveau manner with neurotic linear patterns which evoke recollections of movement, not through the composition being such as to necessitate ocular movement before it is intelligible ... The reason is that the spatial arrangement corresponds fundamentally to the actual movements of the man who inhabits it; organic architecture is not abstractly utilitarian but, in the integral sense of the word, functional. We are still too much in the habit of looking at a house as though it were a picture, and even the best critics are often better at analysing plans and sections and elevations than the total structure and the spatial conception of a building. The organic architect concentrates upon the structure, and he regards it not merely from a technical point of view but as the complex of all the human activities and feelings of the people who will use it.
>
> Architecture is organic when the spatial arrangement of room, house and city is planned for human happiness, material, psychological and spiritual. The organic is based therefore on a social idea and not on a figurative idea. We can only call architecture organic when it aims at being human before it is humanist.
> Bruno Zevi, *Towards an Organic Architecture* [17]

Organicism in various guises was a major theme in modern architecture long before its critical capacity was polemically re-asserted by the Italian critic Bruno Zevi in the years immediately following the Second World War. Nature, rather than history, had certainly been an inspiration for designers and aesthetic theorists throughout the second half of the 19th century, making itself manifest in such diverse phenomena as John Ruskin's alpine romanticism as we find this in his *Stones of Venice* of 1853, or Eugène Viollet-le-Duc's excursus on the structure of Mont Blanc, or in Owen Jones' *Grammar of Ornament* of 1856, where Jones sets forth a system for devising new ornamentation from botanical forms. Hence the chestnut of leaves which were included as a potential source for patterns deriving from nature among the plates of his illuminated encyclopedia of ornament. Here we have the imbrication of nature as the demi-urge, combined with an ethnographic-cum-archeological overview, since over two-thirds of Jones' ornament was drawn from non-Eurocentric sources – from Egypt, Greece, Africa, India, China, Japan and from the world of Islam in general. Jones' Orientalizing compendium is obviously the inspiration behind the American architect Louis Sullivan's *A System of Architectural Ornament According to the Philosophy of Men's Powers*, first published in 1924, the year of his death. Apart from geometricizing Jones' basic principle, Sullivan had been specifically inspired in his ornamental design by Asa Gray's *Elements of Botany* of 1836, just as the Dutch architect Hendrik Petrus Berlage would derive much of his ornament for the Amsterdam Stock Exchange of 1903 from Ernst Hackel's *Kunstformen der Natur* of 1899. Thus we touch in passing on the *raison d'être* of the Art Nouveau in general; namely that since tradition had degenerated into eclecticism there was little choice but to turn to *nature* as the one emerging universal source in which to find renewed vitality and significance. Hence the sycamore "seed germ" posited as the ultimate source of all ornamental form in Sullivan's thesis, and the importance of the transformations in organic morphology analyzed in D'Arcy Thompson's scientific treatise *On Growth and Form*, first published in 1917. This last would exert a latent influence on architectural culture throughout the first half of the 20th century, above all on the career of the Danish architect Jørn Utzon whose concept of additive architecture was based on a cellular paradigm, as we find this in the stepped incremental form of the prefabricated concrete aisles of his Bagsvaerd Church, realized in 1976 at Copenhagen (Fig. 43).

When we look back over the trajectory of the century, we may readily identify three separate strands in the evolution of an organic building culture. In the first place there is the protean figure of Frank Lloyd Wright, who would never tire of proclaiming his work as the ultimate manifestation of *organicism*; in the second, there is the image of a liberative crystalline form as this is evoked in the visionary writings of the German anarchic poet Paul Scheerbart, whose prose-poem *Glasarchitektur* of 1914 was to become the primary source for German Expressionism in architecture, inspiring a continuous trajectory of development that runs from the earliest works of

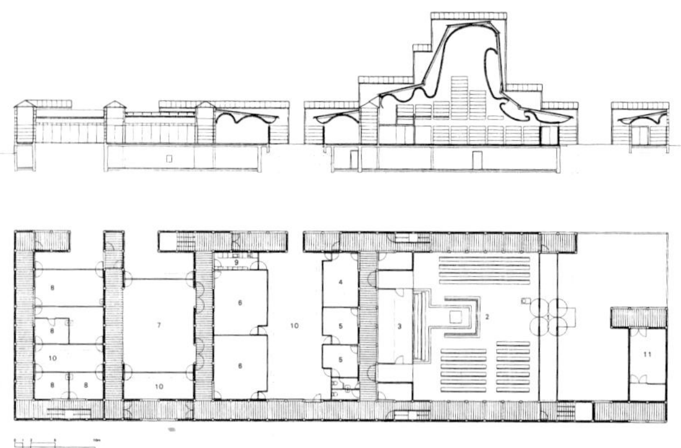

Fig. 43 Jørn Utzon, Bagsvaerd Church, near Copenhagen, Denmark. 1976. Plan & section.

Hans Scharoun and Hugo Häring through to the much later achievements of the German architect Günter Benisch. Last but not least there is the Finnish architect Alvar Aalto, whose work was also permeated by an impulse that was fundamentally organic.

2.1 Frank Lloyd Wright and the Cause Conservative 1893–1959

While it is difficult to define organic architecture in an absolute sense, it is rather clear that it was, at bottom, not only opposed to the vernacular and classical traditions, but also to the *tabula rasa* aims of the abstract, anti-natural culture of the artistic avant-garde. Wright, for his part, would see the organic as "dedicated to the cause conservative in the best sense of the word." By a similar token he would assert that the organic was inseparable from its profound roots in the Orient. For him it was to be found, above all, in the philosophy of Lao-tzu, although as we know, traditional Japanese culture, as embodied in the prints of Hokusai, was to have a decisive impact on his transformation of the Anglo-Saxon Arts and Crafts tradition (c.f. his relationship to the work of Voysey) into the so-called Prairie Style as this was set forth in his Wasmuth Volumes, published in Berlin in 1910. Wrights's first encounter with Japanese architecture in the flesh was the Ho-o-den Temple that had been erected by the Japanese government for the World's Columbia Exhibition staged at Chicago in 1893. This diminutive manifestation of a totally "other" architecture seems to have had a particularly profound influence on his early development, as we may judge from Grant Carpenter Manson's perceptive study, *Frank Lloyd Wright to 1910*:

> If we assume that actual confrontation with Japanese building was the necessary mechanism required at a certain juncture in his career to give those concepts reality and direction, then many of the steps in the evolution of his architecture can be rationally explained. As examples: the translation of the *tokonoma*, the permanent element of a Japanese interior and the focus of domestic contemplation and ceremony, into its Western counterpart, the fireplace, but a fireplace expanded to unprecedented, animistic importance; the frank revelation of the masonry of the fireplace and chimney as the one desired solid substance in an architecture of ever-increasing movement; the opening out of the interior spaces away from the chimney-breast towards shifting planes of glass at their further limits; the extension of the great eaves beyond these planes to modify and control the intensity of light which they admit and to protect them from weather; the subdivision of interior space by suggestion rather than partition, acknowledging and accommodating the fluctuating human uses to which it is put; the elimination of all sculptured and varnished trim in favor of flat surfaces and natural wood-all these and more could have been adduced from the lesson of the Ho-o-den.[18]

It was to take Wright another eight years to integrate certain aspects drawn from the Japanese tradition with the legacy of the Arts and Crafts, thereby creating that unique lowrise, horizontal domestic manner with which he was to express the myth of the Prairie. This came with his *Ladies Home Journal* house of 1901 and his famous address "The Art and Craft of the Machine" of the same year, in which he argued that modern wood-working machinery would enable us "to wipe out the mass of meaningless torture to which wood has been subjected since the world began... by all peoples except the Japanese." There followed in 1908 his masterly Avery Coonley House in Riverside, Illinois and his first essay under the title "In the Cause of Architecture" wherein we read:

> A sense of the organic is indispensable to an architect ... A knowledge of the relations of form and function lies at the root of his practice; where else can he find the pertinent object lessons Nature so readily furnishes? Where can he study the differentiations of form that go to determine character as he can study them in trees? ...
>
> Japanese art knows this school more intimately than that of any other people. In common use in their language there are many words like the word *edaburi* which, translated as near as may be, means the formative arrangement of the branches of a tree. We have no such word in English, we are not sufficiently civilized to think in such terms ... We of the Middle West are living on the prairie. The prairie has a beauty of its own, and we should recognize and accentuate this natural beauty, its quiet level. Hence, gentle sloping roofs, low proportions, quiet skylines, suppressed heavyset chimneys and sheltering overhangs, low terraces and out-reaching walls sequestering private gardens ...
>
> Colors require the same conventionalizing process to make them fit to live with that natural forms do; so go to the woods and the fields for color schemes. Use the soft warm, optimistic tones of earth and autumn leaves ... Bring out the nature of the materials, let their nature intimately into your scheme. Strip the wood of varnish and let it alone - stain it ... Reveal the nature of wood, plaster, brick or stone in your designs, they are all by nature friendly and beautiful ...
>
> Above all integrity. The machine is the normal tool of our civilization, give it work that it can do well – nothing is of greater importance. To do this will formulate new industrial ideals, sadly needed.[19]

Many things are evident from this passage that are important keys to Wright's particular concept of the organic, including the view that an organic architecture is in no way inimical to the methods and constraints of machine production. Wright conceived of his buildings as poetic mechanisms without in any way idealizing the machine as an end in itself. This was as true of Wright's canonical Larkin Building of 1906, designed as an "information machine", as for any of his do-

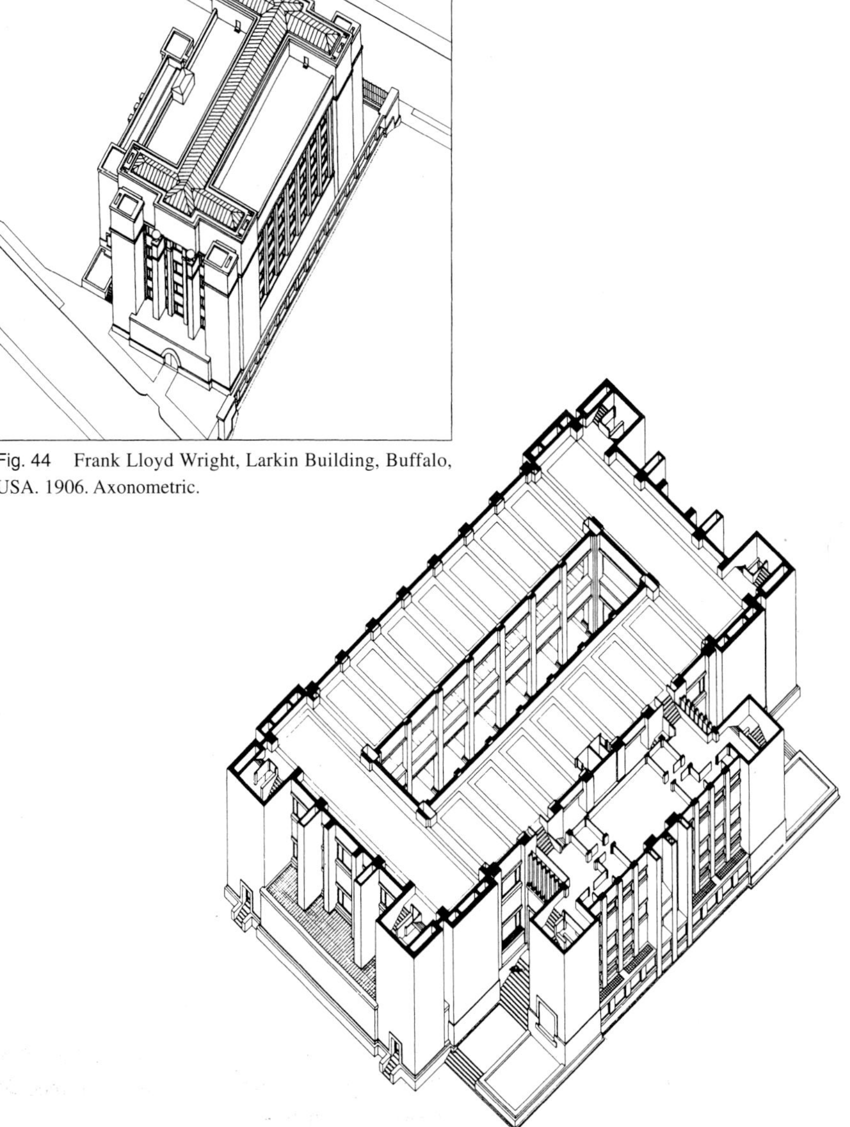

Fig. 44 Frank Lloyd Wright, Larkin Building, Buffalo, USA. 1906. Axonometric.

Fig. 45 Frank Lloyd Wright, Larkin Building, Buffalo, USA. 1906. Cutaway axonometric.

mestic buildings, Wright being ever inclined to render both the workplace and the home as complementary spiritual domains (Figs. 44 & 45). This is unequivocally the case in the Larkin Building which, apart from the pipe organ that presided over its five story, top-lit atrium, was also embellished with morally uplifting inscriptions such as, "Seek and Ye Shall Find," "Knock and It Shall Be Opened Unto You," along with fourteen sets of three inspirational words of which the client William Heath wrote: "Simple words were inscribed rather than great quotations because they permit independence of thought and individuality of interpretation ... "

The Martin Mail Order Co, the client for the Larkin Building, conceived of itself as a paternalistically benevolent institution, as much concerned with the welfare of its staff, in every sense, as with the prosperity of the company. This would be just as true with Johnson Wax Corporation 33 years later, when Wright effectively re-worked the Larkin concept in the S.C. Johnson Administration Building, completed in Racine, Wisconsin in 1939 for his enlightened industrialist client, Herbert Johnson (Figs. 46 & 47). This luminous, muted, streamlined introspective complex took Wright's concept of the organic to another level, engendering one of the unsurpassed masterpieces of 20th century architecture-possibly the most sublime artistic work that North America has produced to date. Moreover, this is the only monument of the epoch capable of standing comparison, as Wright always intended, to the finest monuments of "world culture" produced over the entirety of time.

Here, consciously or otherwise, the model was not so much Japanese as it was Islamic, with the 60 lily pad, concrete mushroom columns of the Johnson Wax workroom resembling nothing so much as the columns subdividing the open volume of a vast mosque. Like the Larkin Building, the Johnson Wax office complex was a totally introspective structure, stepping back at the roof level and clad in fair-faced brickwork throughout with raked horizontal joints. The resulting linear treatment imparted a sweeping, streamlined character to the exterior that was further emphasized by the hollow "anti-cornice" at the top of the second floor together with the ground floor clerestory, each translucent band being fabricated out of horizontally stacked glass tubing, with caulked seams. This same translucent material was used for the interstitial roof lights between the flat, circular column heads, the roof being rendered watertight through the provision of a second, more conventional skylight above. Like the Larkin Building this was once again a woven tectonic fabric with each element interpenetrating the next in a structure that was quite literally made up of a "warp" and a "weft", operating at different interlocking scales. Typically enough Wright was to stretch the limits of current building technology in this work, from his unprecedented use of glass tubing to the casting of heating pipes into the concrete floor slabs; from his pioneering use of high-strength concrete to the application of wire-mesh reinforcement to sustain the hollow lily pads, these last being hollow so as to serve not only to support the roof but also to drain it (Fig. 48)

Fig. 46 Frank Lloyd Wright, S. C. Johnson Administration Building, Racine, Wisconsin, USA. 1936–39. Interior.

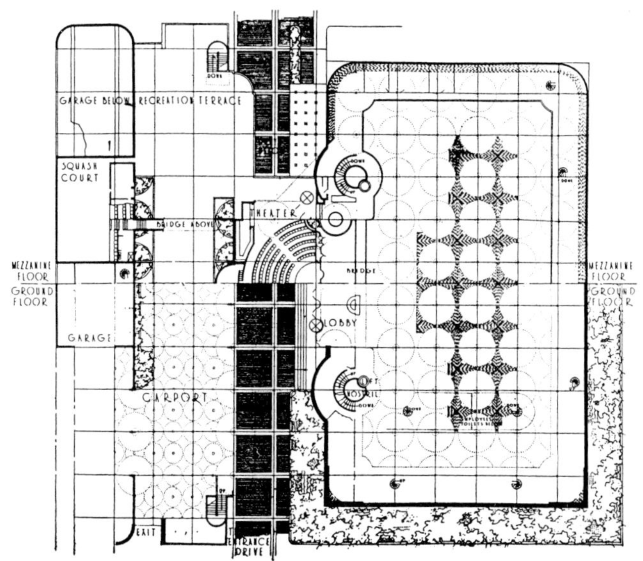

Fig. 47 Frank Lloyd Wright, S. C. Johnson Administration Building, Racine, Wisconsin, USA. 1936–39. Plan.

This work, which was the crowning achievement of Wright's Usonian period in the late 30s, was matched by two other organic innovations. The first of these was his advocacy of low-rise regional urbanization, his so-called Broadacre City (1934) which, according to his omnipotent

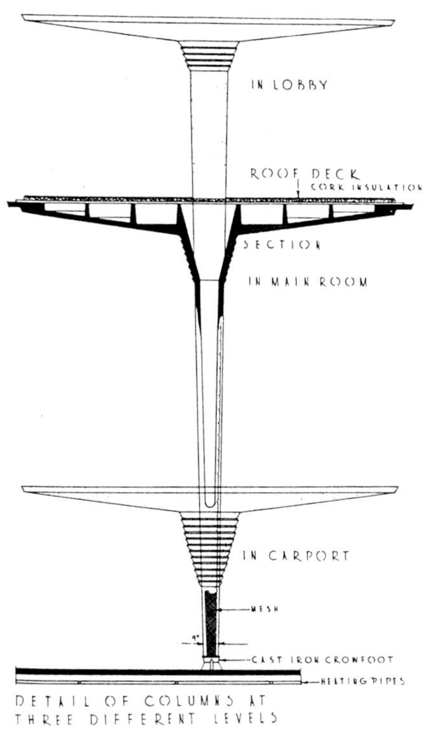

Fig. 48 Frank Lloyd Wright, S. C. Johnson Administration Building, Racine, Wisconsin, USA. 1936–39. Section through hollow columns.

fantasies, would have been based on the reservation of an acre of fertile land for every American at birth (Fig. 49). The resulting agrarian-cum-manufacturing economy envisaged for Broadacre City was in fact an updating of Peter Kropotkin's *Factories, Fields and Workshops* of 1898 and was, in this respect, close to similar decentralizing urban theses advanced in the Soviet Union at virtually the same time. Like N.A. Milutin's linear city thesis of 1930, Broadacre was based upon automotive distribution, machine production and electronic telecommunications. As Wright put it in 1935, in his habitual apodictic manner, "It is in the nature of universal electrification that the city should not exist."

The second innovation, of greater and more practical consequence, was Wright's model of the Usonian house, perfected in the single-story Stanley Rosenbaum residence, completed in Florence, Alabama in 1939 (Fig. 50). This house, L-shaped in plan, was in effect a courtyard dwelling, with

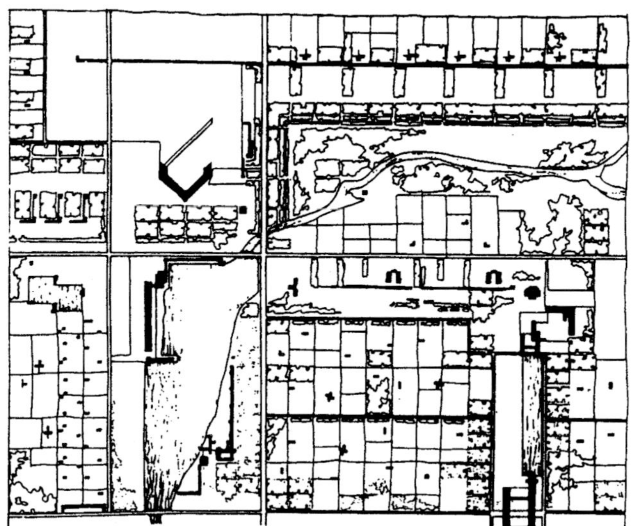

Fig. 49 Frank Lloyd Wright, Broadacre City. 1934. Plan.

its living and bedroom wings facing respectively south and west towards a paved terrace and a garden. The Rosenbaum prototype was entered through a carport, where the two wings met at the service hub of the house comprising a kitchen, a bathroom and a heating chamber. In this generic type, the kitchen invariably opened directly onto a dining alcove that in its turn gave onto a living space and a garden terrace with a study situated at the end of the living volume. In the Rosenbaum version the largely opaque north wall to the street was lined with bookshelves. Based on a 2 x 4 foot module it was built entirely of standard timber, scantlings and sheets, save for the concrete podium and the occasional brick wall and chimney shaft. Once again as in the S.C. Johnson building the space was heated by continuous copper tubing cast into the concrete floor slab. Wright's introduction of a red dye into the aggregate transformed the bare concrete into a richly colored floor surface that could be maintained through wax polishing.

The accessibility and realizability of this paradigm (Wright was to build well over 200 Usonian Houses between 1932 and 1959) suggests that Wright's Usonian house was the last serious effort to render the North American suburb as a place of civility. Wright with great prescience proclaimed that America would not need to help Broadacre City, "for it will haphazardly build itself." This has long since proven to be not only the most perspicacious but also the most tragic of his many prophetic utterances, since although suburban development now covers much of the North American continent it can hardly be said to correspond to the idealism of Broadacre vision.

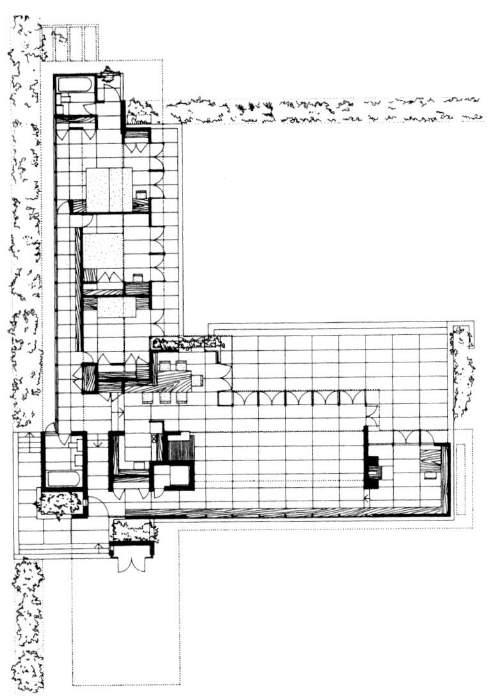

Fig. 50 Frank Lloyd Wright, Rosenbaum House, Florence, Alabama, USA. 1939. Plan.

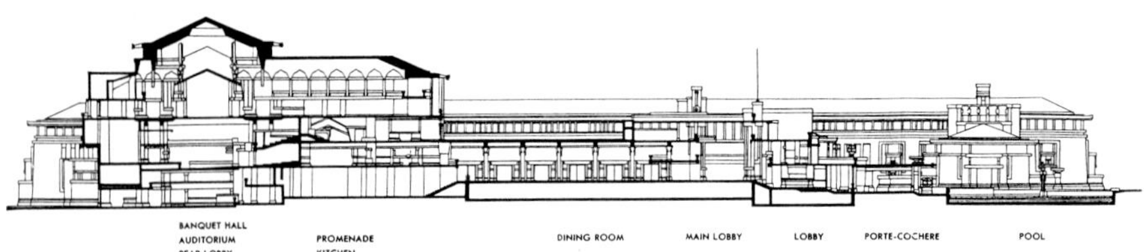

Fig. 51 Frank Lloyd Wright, Imperial Hotel, Tokyo, Japan. 1917–23. Section.

Wright exercised a powerful if somewhat recalcitrant influence on world architecture throughout his life. This influence was disseminated in part through his most talented assistants of the Prairie Style period, that is to say the period extending from the first Ladies Home Journal house of 1901 to the Imperial Hotel, Tokyo completed at the end of 1922 (Fig. 51). Three of his assistants from this era inaugurated their own careers during the first quarter of the century, transferring their version of the Wrightian message to the other side of the world. The first two of these were Marion Mahoney and her husband Walter Burley Griffin, who left Wright's employment in 1912,

Fig. 52 Antonin Raymond, Otis Elevator Factory, Tokyo, Japan. 1932.

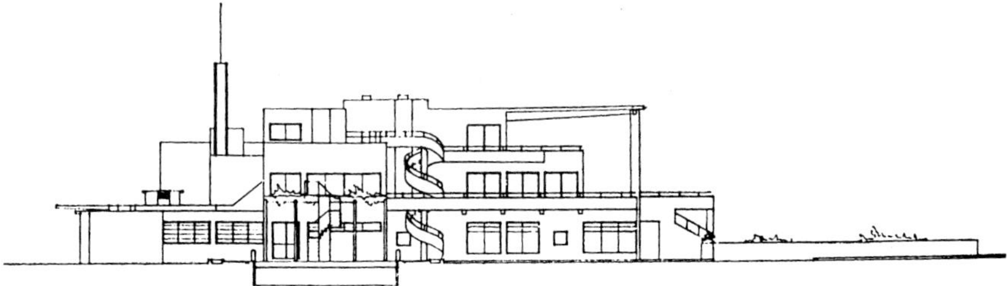

Fig. 53 Antonin Raymond, Tokyo Golf Club, Saitama, Tokyo, Japan. 1930. Elevation.

after winning the Canberra, Australian Capitol competition of that year. The other seminal figure was the Czech émigré Antonin Raymond, who, having served as the site architect for the Imperial Hotel, set up on his own in Tokyo in 1923, going on to realize such canonical works as the Otis Elevator Factory (1932) (Fig. 52), and the Tokyo Golf Club (1930) (Fig. 53); buildings which were to exercise an influence on the evolution of modern Japanese architecture right up to the military seizure of power in Tokyo in 1936 and Raymond's enforced departure.

2.2 In the Wrightian Vein 1910–1959

The next generation to be launched through their apprenticeship with Wright were the Austrian émigrés Rudolf Schindler and Richard Neutra, who through their joint and independent practices in Los Angeles, greatly enriched the Southern Californian modern tradition that had been initiated by the Greene Brothers and their Japanesque architecture built in Pasadena around 1906, along with Irving Gill's pioneering abstract architecture in reinforced concrete, as embodied in his

Dodge House of 1916. Schindler's own King's Road house in Los Angeles of 1922 employed a version of the tilt slab concrete system pioneered by Gill (Fig. 54 & 55). This plus Schindler's twelve-unit El Pueblo Ribera courtyard house complex (Fig. 56), completed in La Jolla in 1925, not only paved the way for Neutra's parallel career but also anticipated, in certain aspects, the evolution of Wright's Usonian house that would come some 16 years later. Neutra, for his part, would virtually invent the white, dematerialized International Style overnight with his steel-framed Lovell House completed in 1929 on a romantic site overlooking Griffith Park, Los Angeles (Fig. 57).

Neutra's progressive, lightweight systematic approach to both building and landscape, evident from his Corona Bell School (1935) and his low-rise, high-density Strathmore Apartments (1938), (Figs. 58 & 59) had a lasting impact on Southern Californian architects, some of whom served their initial apprenticeship under him, among them Gregory Ain, Rafael Soriano and Harwell Hamilton Harris, who together with H.R.Davidson, made up the so-called "second generation" of Southern Califor-

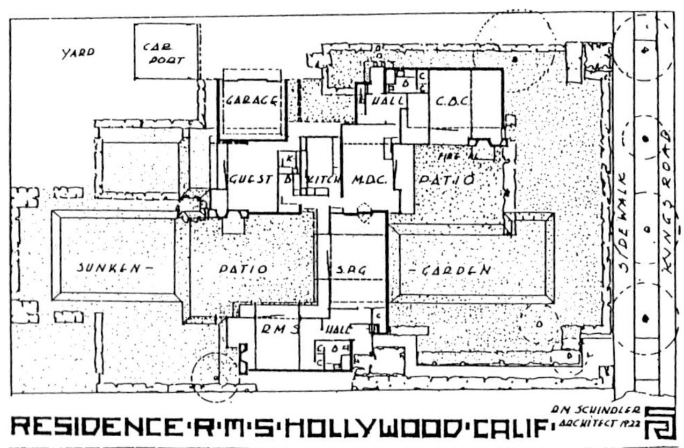

Fig. 54 Rudolf Schindler, King's Road House, Los Angeles, California, USA. 1921–22. Plan.

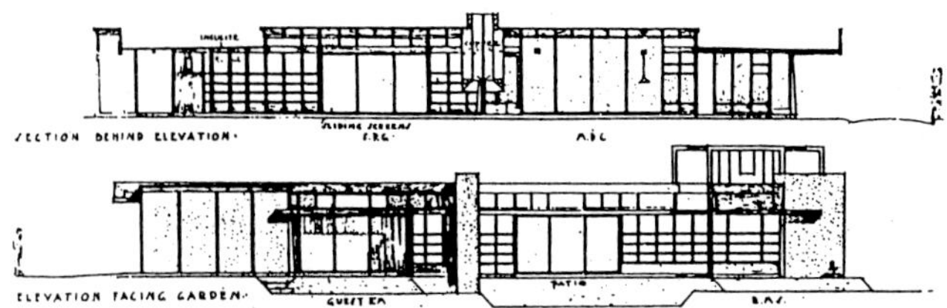

Fig. 55 Rudolf Schindler, King's Road House, Los Angeles, California, USA. 1921–22. Section and elevation.

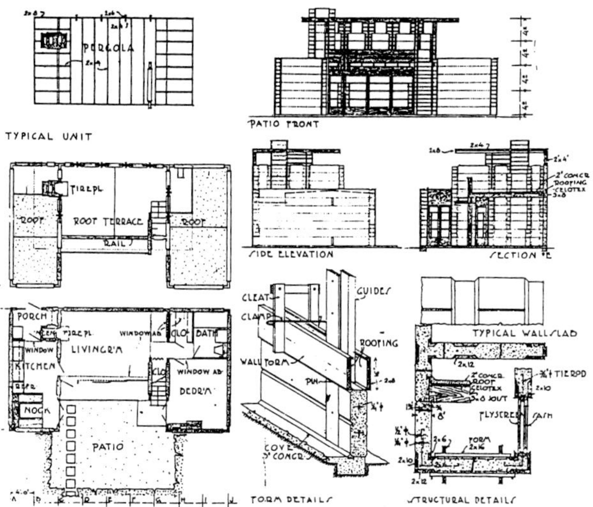

Fig. 56 Rudolf Schindler, Pueblo Ribera Courtyard Housing, La Jolla, California, USA. 1923–25. Typical unit plus constructional details.

Fig. 57 Richard Neutra, Lovell House, Griffith's Park, Los Angeles, California, USA. 1927.

nian architects. From these men followed the third generation among whom were Pierre Koenig, Craig Ellwood, and above all Charles and Ray Eames, (Fig. 60) architects who would make their initial mark with John Entenza's Case Study House Program which effectively sponsored a whole series of prototypical modern houses in Southern California between the mid-50s and the early 60s.

Over the same trajectory, something of Wright's influence could also be discerned in the American Art Deco movement. It was surely evident in Raymond Hood's Rockefeller Center, New York

Fig. 58 Richard Neutra, Strathmore Apartments, Los Angeles, California, USA. 1938.

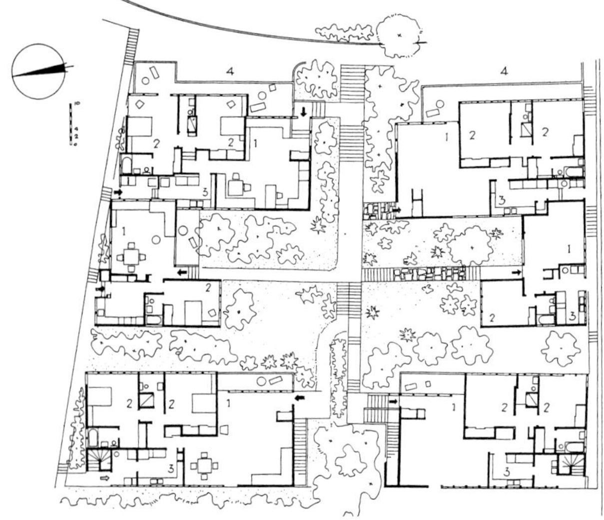

Fig. 59 Richard Neutra, Strathmore Apartments, Los Angeles, California, USA. 1938. Plan.

(1932–39) (Fig. 61), which may have been rhythmically and tectonically related to Wright's National Life Insurance project of 1924 (Fig. 62). Going beyond this point in time into the post-1945 era we may even claim that the "servant versus served" principle, so patently in evidence in Wright's Larkin Building of 1906, was reinterpreted in the ventilaition shafts and stair towers of Louis Kahn's Richards Laboratories, completed in 1959, the year of Wright's death.

As we have seen, Wright's impact on Europe begins with the publication of his Wasmuth Volumes in 1910, his Prairie Style being immediately transformed into the cubistic abstractions of the Neoplastic movement and into the contrapuntal brick masses of the Berlage School, not to men-

Fig. 60 Charles and Ray Eames, Eames House, Pacific Palisades, Los Angeles, California, USA. 1943–49.

Fig. 61 Raymond Hood and Associated Architects, Rockefeller Center, New York, USA. 1932–39.

tion W.M.Dudok's Hilversum Town Hall and his De Bijenkorf department store, both dating from 1930 (Fig. 63). Last but not least, Wright is certainly present in the early work of Walter Gropius and Mies van der Rohe, in Gropius and Meyer's Werkbund Administration building of 1914 and in Mies's Brick Country House project of 1923.

Wright's latter-day influence in Europe will be evident after 1945, particularly, at the detailed syntactical level, above all in the Italian Neo-Liberty work of Carlo Scarpa, Franco Aibini and Leonardo de Ricci and more typologically perhaps in the Danish architect Jørn Utzon's Kingo Courtyard housing of 1956 (Figs. 64 & 65). This last combined Wright's L-shaped Usonian House, with a site plan drawn from Clarence Stein and Henry Wright's model community of Radburn

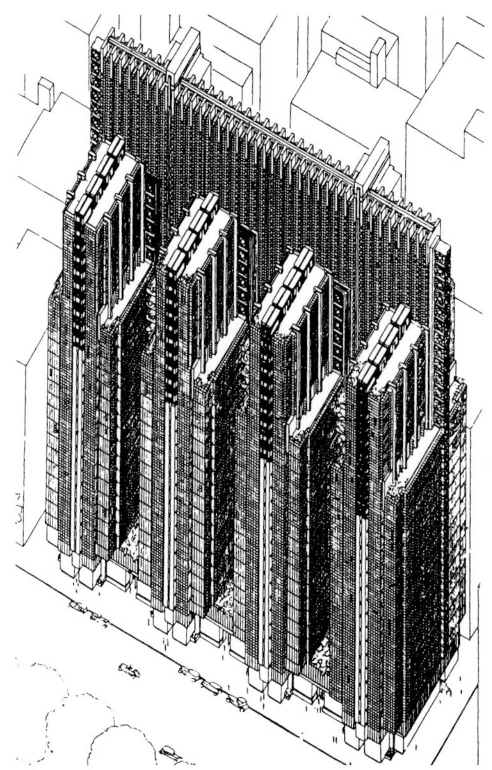

Fig. 62 Frank Lloyd Wright, National Life Insurance, Chicago, Illinois, USA. 1924. Axonometric.

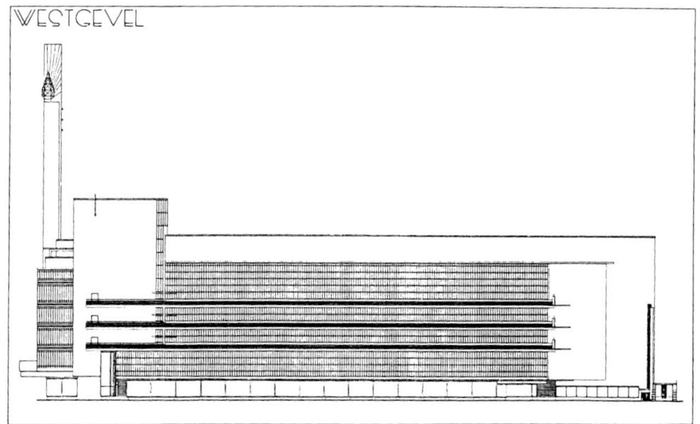

Fig. 63 W. M. Dudok, De Bijenkorf, Rotterdam, Holland. 1930. West elevation.

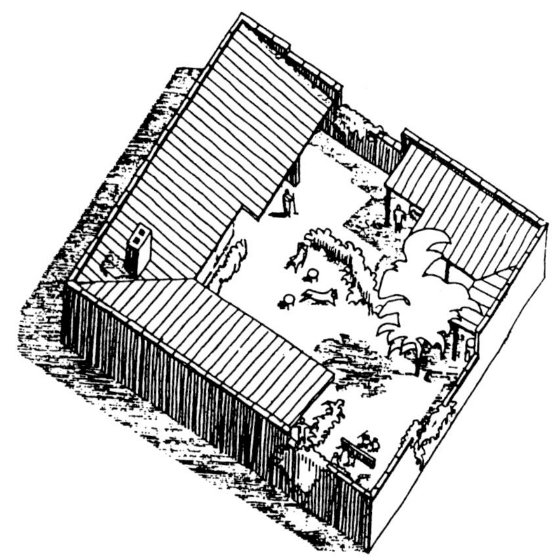

Fig. 64 Jørn Utzon, Kingo Housing, near Helsingnør, Denmark. 1956. Prototypical unit.

Fig. 65 Jørn Utzon, Kingo Housing, near Helsingnør, Denmark. 1956. Site plan.

realized at Fair Lawn, New Jersey, U.S.A. in 1926. Finally there is a noticeable Wrightian influence in the Ticino region of Switzerland in the 1950s, evident in the early work of such architects such as Rino Tami, Tita Carloni, Peppo Brevio and Luigi Snozzi.

2.3 European Expressionism: From the Crystal Chain to Coop Himmelblau 1901–1998

Prefigured in the 1901 inaugural rite of the artist's colony in Darmstadt, wherein a symbolic crystal was borne up the steps of Josef Maria Olbrich's studio building, the concept of the crystalline as the source of universal harmony was advanced in two visionary works published and realized in 1914 on the eve of the First World War; Paul Scheerbart's prose-poem *Glasarchitektur* and Bruno Taut's glass pavilion built for the Deutsche Werkbund exhibition of that year. Where the one imagined a redemptive, anarchic utopia, constructed entirely of steel and colored glass, the other demonstrated a parallel vision in the form of a largely translucent pavilion displaying the latest products of the German glass industry (Fig. 66). This faceted, all but conical, ferro-vitreous structure coincidentally represented the form of some unspecified cult building capable of redeeming the Gesellschaft of Wihelmine Germany.

Scheerbart's *Glasarchitektur* was dedicated to Taut, whose glass pavilion was in turn inscribed with Scheerbartian slogans: "Light wants crystal"; "Glass brings a new era"; "We feel sorry for the brick culture"; "Without a glass palace, life becomes a burden", "Building in brick only does us harm", "Colored glass destroys hatred". This last slogan referred to the light that filtered through the faceted cupola and glass block walls of Taut's Pavilion to illuminate a seven-tiered chamber lined with glass mosaics. One rose to a platform under the dome and then descended on either side of a stepped fountain. According to Taut this crystalline structure had been designed in the spirit of a Gothic cathedral. It approximated in fact to a "city crown", that pyramidal form postu-

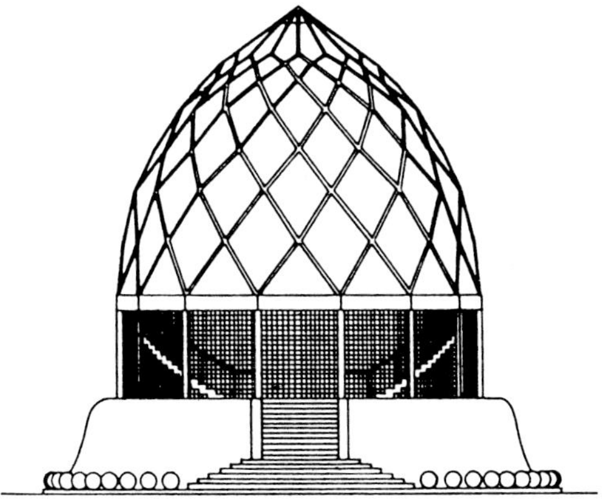

Fig. 66 Bruno Taut, Glass Pavilion, Deutsche Werkbund Exhibition, Cologne, Germany. 1914. Elevation.

lated by Taut in his book *Die Stadtkrone* of 1919 as being the universal paradigm of all religious building which, together with the faith it would inspire, was seen as an essential element for the restructuring of society.

With the armistice of November 1918, Taut began to organize the anarcho-socialist *Arbeitsrat für Kunst* movement which declared its basic aims in Taut's *Architekturprogramm* of December 1918, which argued for a new total work of art, to be created with the active participation of the people. Led by Taut and Walter Gropius, *the Arbeitsrat für Kunst* comprised some 50 artists and patrons living in and around Berlin, including the architects Otto Bartning, Max Taut, Bernhard Hoetger, Adolf Meyer, and Erich Mendelsohn. In April 1919, these last staged an exhibition of visionary works under the title "An Exhibition of Unknown Architects". In his introduction to the exhibition Gropius wrote:

> Painters, sculptors, break down the barriers around architecture and become co-builders and comrades-in-arms towards art's ultimate goal: the creative idea of the Cathedral of the Future [*Zukunftskathedrale*], which will once more encompass everything in *one* form – architecture and sculpture and painting. [20]

This call for a new religious building, capable of unifying the creative energy of the society as in the Middle Ages became in effect the Weimar Bauhaus program, published in the same month.

The suppression of the Spartacist Revolt in 1919 put an end to the activities of the *Arbeitsrat für Kunst*, and the energies of the group were channeled into a series of letters known as the "Crystal Chain". This was Bruno Taut's so-called "Utopian Correspondence", which began in November 1919 after Taut's suggestion that "everyone of us will draw or write down at brief intervals of time, informally and as the spirit moves him... those ideas which he would like to share with our circle". The correspondence involved some fourteen artists and architects. Apart from Taut, who called himself *Glas*, there was Gropius (*Mass*), Finsterlin (*Prometh*), and Bruno Taut's brother Max who employed the cryptic pseudonym *kein name;* no name! This inner circle was complemented by architects who had previously only had a peripheral involvement with the worker's council, notably the brothers Hans and Wassili Luckhardt and Hans Scharoun.

By 1920, however, the bond between the various members of the chain began to weaken, beginning with Hans Luckhardt's sober recognition that free form and rational prefabricated production were incompatible. While Luckhardt's rationalism had the effect of returning the debate to the issues that had divided the Werkbund in 1914, Taut continued to assert the "crystal" utopian theme in his books *Alpine Architektur* and *Die Stadtkrone* and in *Die Auflösung der Städte* "The

Dissolution of Cities", published in 1920. In common with the socialist planners of the Russian Revolution, Taut recommended the break-up of cities and the return of the urbanized population to the land. At his most practical, he attempted to formulate models for agrarian and handicraft-based communities; at his most fantastic, he projected glass-enclosed religious retreats in the Alps. However, it was not Taut but Hans Poelzig who was first to realize the image of the "city crown" in three dimensions. This was the interior of the 5,000-seat theater that he designed for Max Reinhardt in Berlin in 1919 which came closer to Scheerbart's original vision than any post-war achievement by Taut (Fig. 67).

After establishing himself as an architect in Breslau in 1911, Poelzig realized two works which seem to have influenced the subsequent formal language adopted by Erich Mendelsohn. These were a water tower for Posen and an office building in Breslau. This last seems to have suggested the format of Mendelsohn's *Berliner-Tageblatt* building on which Richard Neutra worked before migrating to the United States in 1923. Mendelsohn would realize his own version of Taut's "city crown" in the observatory that he realized for Albert Einstein at Potsdam in 1921 (Fig. 68) while strongly influenced by Taut's glass pavilion of 1914, the Einstein Tower also displayed a certain

Fig. 67 Hans Poelzig, Schauspielhaus, Berlin, Germany. 1919. Perspective.

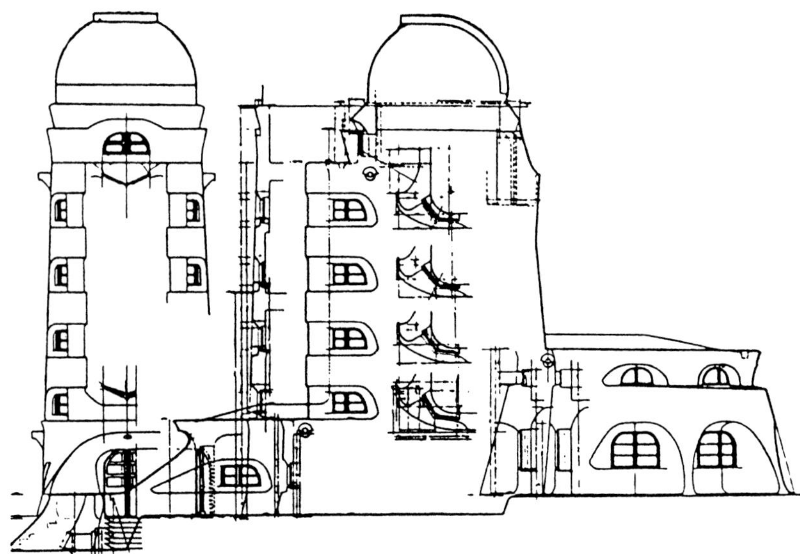

Fig. 68 E. Mendelsohn, Einstein Tower, Potsdam, Germany. 1921. Half plan plus elevations.

affinity with Dutch Expressionism, a movement centered around Theo van Wijdeveld's magazine *Wendingen* (Turnings). Soon after the completion of the observatory Mendelsohn was invited to Holland by Wijdeveld to see the work of the *Wendingen* circle for himself. In Amsterdam he visited a number of Expressionist housing schemes which were then under construction, as part of Berlage's plan for Amsterdam South, including Michel de Klerk's Eigen Haard (1913–19) and Piet Kramer's De Dageraad (1918–23). Outside the Amsterdam School of Wijdeveld, De Klerk and Kramer, Mendelsohn met and was influenced by a number of other Dutch architects of a rather different persuasion, above all the rationalist Rotterdam architect J.J.P. Oud and the Wrightian architect W.M. Dudok, practicing in Hilversum. Mendelsohn would be strongly influenced by the structural expressiveness of the Amsterdam School, as one may judge from a hat factory that he built at Luckenwalde in 1923, where the pitched-roofed production sheds were modeled in a manner reminiscent of De Klerk (Fig. 69). These stood in strong contrast to the smooth, flat-roofed powerhouse whose layered "cubist" expression in brick and concrete recalled the early works of Dudok. The principle established here, of setting dramatic tall industrial forms against horizontal administrative elements, was repeated by Mendelsohn in his unbuilt Leningrad textile mill projected in 1925. In this instance, however, a further step was taken, for the banded modeling of the administration block anticipated the profiling of his Schocken department stores, to be built in Breslau, Stuttgart, Chemnitz and Berlin between 1927 and 1931 (Fig.70).

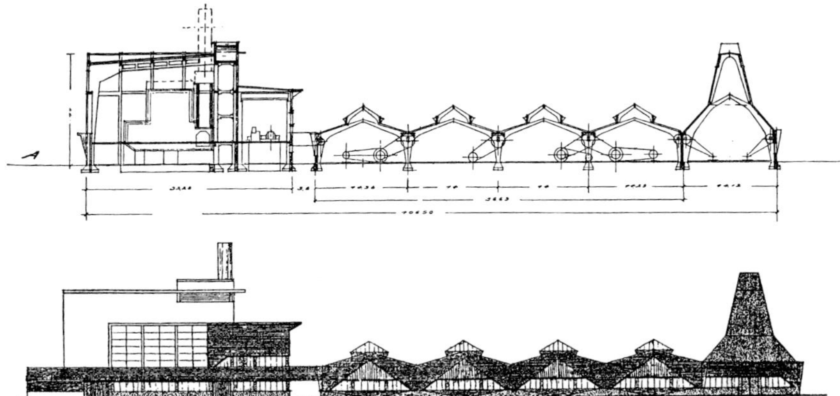

Fig. 69 E. Mendelsohn, Hat Factory, Luckenwalde, Germany. 1921–23. Section and elevations.

Fig. 70 E.Mendelsohn, Schocken Department Store, Chemnitz, Germany. 1928–29.

In the farm complex that Hugo Häring realized near Lübeck in 1924 (Fig. 71), we find a similar structural expressiveness, with single and double pitched roofs set in opposition to brick masses with rounded corners. Although Häring, like Mendelsohn, believed in the primacy of function, he sought to transcend mere utility by deriving his forms from a more sensitive analysis of the program. Like Scharoun, Häring's attitude to massing was often imitative of biological form as in Scharoun's Home and Work Exhibition building realized at Breslau in 1928. (Fig. 72) Häring was equally preoccupied with the inner source of form, which he termed the *Organwerk* or the programmatic essence of the building as opposed to its surface expression or *Gestaltwerk*.

Fig. 71 Hugo Häring, Farm, Garkau, Germany. 1924.

Fig. 72 Hans Scharoun, Housing Exhibition, Breslau, Germany. 1929.

Häring's commitment to the organic led him into conflict with Le Corbusier, particularly in the Congrès Internationaux d'Architecture Moderne (CIAM), founded at La Sarraz, Switzerland in 1928. While Le Corbusier proclaimed an architecture of strict functionalism and pure geometry, Häring tried to win over the participants to his more "organic" conception of building. His failure to do so not only presaged the eclipse of the Scheerbartian dream but also a rejection of the place-oriented character of his architecture.

Scharoun's prolific output during the first 40 years of his career far exceeded that of Häring, although few of his realized works from the first half of his career are truly convincing. In fact, only three pieces of compelling quality may be cited from the years 1911–51; the aforementioned Breslau Exhibition building of 1928, the Schminke House, Lobau of 1933 and the Mattern House realized for the landscape architect Mattern at Bornim near Potsdam in 1934. After 1945 Scharoun's debt to Häring will become more explicit, first in the primary school that he projected for Darmstadt in 1951, with its classrooms formally inflected according to the age of the child, and then in the Geschwister Scholl School, completed at Lünen in 1962. Häring's dialectic of the *Organwerk* versus *Gestaltwerk* was brought into play in both instances with the result that these projects, extend themselves into their respective sites as continuously faceted, flowing low-rise forms, compounded of canted roofs and partially enclosed patios.

It is interesting to note how this exfoliating approach could not be convincingly applied to Scharoun's high-rise housing schemes such as the Romeo and Juliet apartment buildings completed at Stuttgart in 1962. However in his low-rise schools and theaters, as in his Haupstadt Berlin competition entry of 1958, Scharoun was able to envisage structures that were so closely integrated with the ground as to constitute a "new nature", just as Bruno Taut's crystalline alpine structures had been

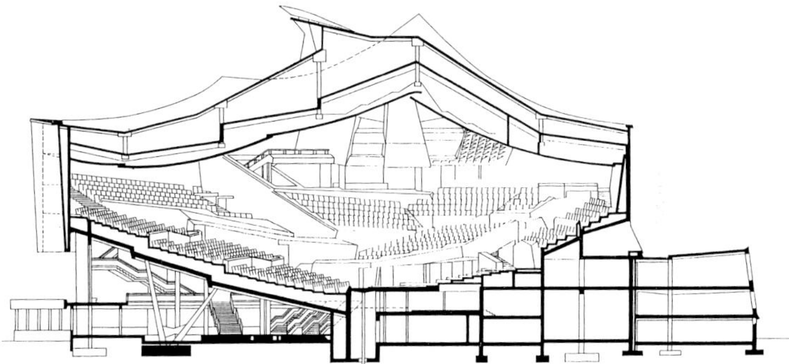

Fig. 73 Hans Scharoun, Philharmonie, Berlin, Germany. 1963. Cross section.

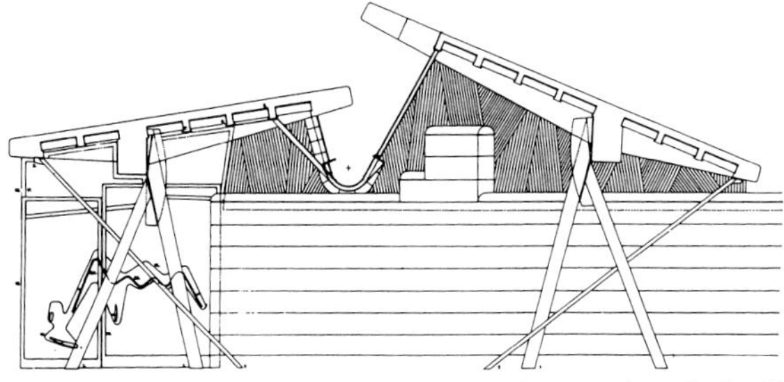

Fig. 74 Enric Miralles and Carme Pinòs, Olympic Archery complex, Barcelona, Spain. 1992. Detail section.

envisaged as extensions of the outcrops on which they were to have been sited.

Taut's idea of the "city crown" finally comes into its own as a free-standing form in Scharoun's masterly Philharmonie concert hall completed in West Berlin in 1963 (Fig. 73). This was Scharoun's famous "music in the middle place", where the orchestra finds itself surrounded on all sides by canted tiers of seats of varying alignment. Scharoun would liken this arrangement to terraced vineyards piling up on the lower slopes of mountain, just as the building itself was conceived as a small mountain or rather, as Margit Staber has suggested, as an iceberg floating in the Baltic which Scharoun would have remembered from his youth in Bremehaven.

Scharoun's influence both before and after his death in 1972 was quite diffuse, extending beyond the confines of his native Germany to include within its orbit the work of the Catalan architects Enric Miralles and Carme Pinòs, in particular their archery complex designed for the Barcelona Olympics in 1992 (Fig. 74) and Frank Gehry's highly rhetorical Guggenheim Museum, completed in Bilbao, Spain in 1997, although here the programmatically organic seems to become overwhelmed by concerns that are exclusively sculptural.

Fig. 75 Günter Behnisch, Olympic Stadium, Munich, Germany. 1972.

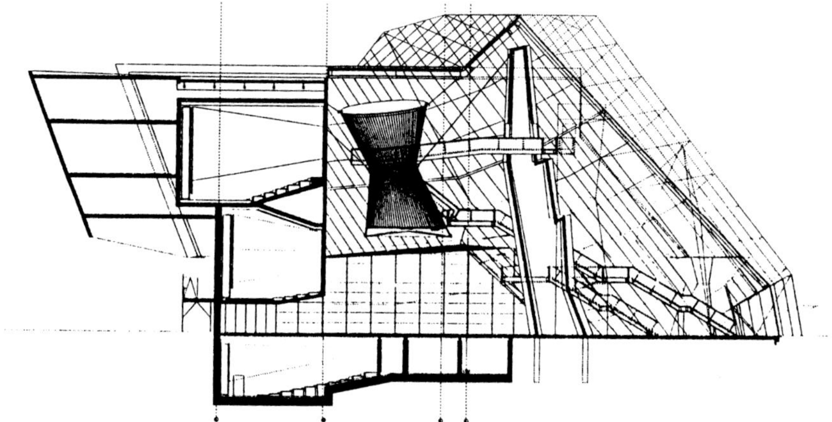

Fig. 76 Coop Himmelblau, Multiplex Cinema, Dresden, Germany. 1993–98. Section.

In Germany, Scharoun's most distinguished follower after 1945 was Günter Benisch and over the years Benisch was to prove himself capable of combining the sociocultural ethos of the organic approach with a more flexible, fine-tuned, ecological mastery of dematerialized building technology, bordering at times on a kind of latter-day Constructivism, such as we find in his Olympic Complex built at Munich in 1972 (Fig. 75) and in the Hysolar Institute realized in Stuttgart in 1987, or the Geschwister Scholl School, completed at Frankfurt-Römerstadt in 1994. Needless to say there were other architects who were touched by Scharoun: among them the Austrian architects Volker Giencke and Coop Himmelblau, as is evident in Giencke's conservatory for Graz of 1995 and Coop Himmelblau's UFA multiplex cinema realized in Dresden in 1998 (Fig. 76). All in all Scharoun would remain a strong influence on Germanic architectural culture throughout the second half of the century, as we may judge from Rudolf Gutbrod's German Pavilion for the 1967 Montreal Expo designed in association with the German master of tent and wire cable construction, the architect / engineer Frei Otto.

2.4 The Biomorphic Architecture of Alvar Aalto 1933–1976

Beginning his career under the rubric of Nordic Classicism and subject in his early maturity to the influence of Scandinavian functionalism, Alvar Aalto did not develop his own organic approach until the early 30s. This first manifested itself in his bent plywood and laminated furniture pieces that went into limited production in 1933. Aalto's new culture of materials, categorically opposed to the Constructivist ethos of chromium-plated bent tubular steel furniture, such as we find in Marcel Breuer's output of the late 20s, first became manifest in the architecture of his own house and studio in the Munkkiniemi suburb of Helsinki in 1936. This house already displayed a number of features that would become typical of his biomorphic manner over the next decade. Inspired in part by the Cubistic collage, this house patently favored fragmentation, layering and multiplicity over the regularity, symmetry and repetition of the Nordic Classical or Functional traditions. We may say that its ultimate origin was the Anglo-Saxon Arts and Crafts house as filtered through the Finnish National Romantic Movement of the 1890s, particularly as this was evident in the *Gesamtkunstwerk* of the painter Akseli Gallén-Kalella and the National Romantic architects, Eliel Saarinen, Herman Gesellius and Armas Lindgren, whose Orientalizing Finnish National pavilion built for the Paris Exhibition of 1900 had, in its turn, been influenced by the neo-Romanesque manner of the American architect H. H. Richardson. What Aalto had in common with this "nationalist" legacy of the turn of the century was a deepening respect for the Finnish forest vernacular, above all for the timber agricultural settlements of Karelia in Eastern Finland, a connection which caused the Finnish critic Gustaf Strengell to speak about Aalto's Munkkiniemi house as the "new Niemala Farm", alluding to the then newly created museum of Finnish vernacular architecture outside Helsinki.

These complex roots account for the material development of Aalto's house in detail, that is to say for the rendering of its L-shaped Arts and Crafts plan as an assembly of shifting, cubistic planes and finishes, including vertical timber siding to the living volume, together with field stone walls and undressed wooden balustrading to the bedroom terrace. This rustic "palette" was offset by white, painted brickwork enclosing the sleeping quarters of the house on three sides.

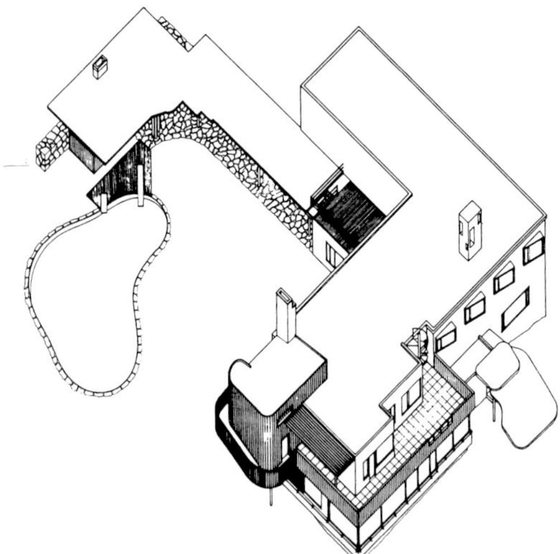

Fig. 77 Alvar Aalto, Villa Mairea, Noormarkku, Finland. 1939. Axonometric.

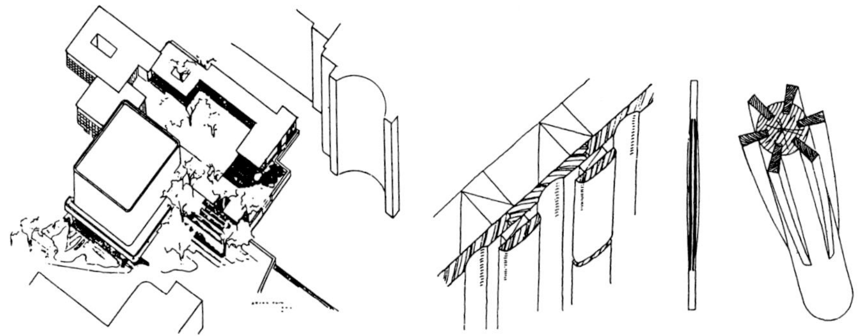

Fig. 78 Alvar Aalto, Finnish Pavilion, World Exhibition, Paris, France. 1937. Axonometric plus details.

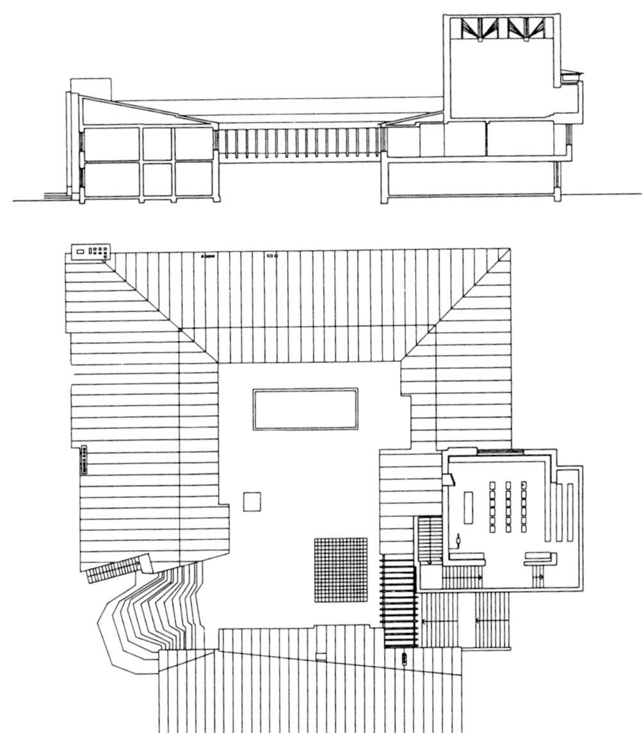

Fig. 79 Alvar Aalto, City Hall, Säynätsalo, Finland. 1949. Plan & section.

Aalto would elaborate and refine this heterotopic formula in his masterly Villa Mairea (1937–39), (Fig. 77) built at Noormarkku for the heiress to the Ahlstrom timber fortune, Maire Gullichsen, who, together with her husband Harry Gullichsen, was an important patron of Aalto's during the 30s and the 40s, commissioning a great deal of industrial work, as well as founding Artek, a firm that was dedicated to the production of his furniture from 1935 up to the present.

Aalto's prize-winning entry for the Finnish Pavilion in the Paris World Exhibition of 1937 (Fig. 78) was a rhetorical display of different techniques of timber construction, each expressing certain characteristics of wood. The battened timber siding of the double-height main hall and the skeleton timber structure of the single-story exhibition space (respectively the head and the tail of a tadpole in the plan) constituted a virtuoso display of Nordic timber technology. Yet for all its technical ingenuity, the importance of the Finnish Pavilion lay in its demonstration of Aalto's site-planning principles, wherein the plan of the building is invariably separated into two distinct elements, and the space between them being articulated as a space for human appearance, as we will find this later not only in the Paris pavilion and the Villa Mairea but also in the brick-clad Saynatsalo Town Hall dating from 1949 (Fig. 79). Aalto was categorically opposed to treating the topography surrounding a building in a decorative manner. He thought that the natural movement of people in and around a building should be exploited as the primary means for shaping the site. Of his Paris exhibition building Aalto wrote:

> One of the most difficult architectural problems is the shaping of the building's surroundings to the human scale. In modern architecture where the rationality of the structural frame and the building masses threaten to dominate, there is often an architectural vacuum in the leftover portions of the site. It would be good if, instead of filling up this vacuum with decorative gardens, the organic movement of people could be incorporated in the shaping of the site in order to create an intimate relationship between Man and Architecture. In the case of the Paris Pavilion, this problem fortunately could be solved. [21]

Aalto was at the height of his powers throughout the 1950s and in one work after another he would demonstrate the full potential of a brick-clad, heterotopic architecture in meeting an extremely broad range of needs in a manner that was at once functional and yet totally integrated into either the urban fabric or the surrounding landscape. The National Pensions Institute and the House of Culture, both realized in Helsinki between 1952 and 1958, plus the Institute of Technology, Otaniemi, (Fig. 80) completed in 1964, were each canonical demonstrations of this topographical approach. While this architecture was unequivocally modern in terms of all its spatial and environmental provisions, it was at the same time broadly accessible to the society at large, particularly to Finland's middle-class, welfare state, suspended in more ways than one between the rigid

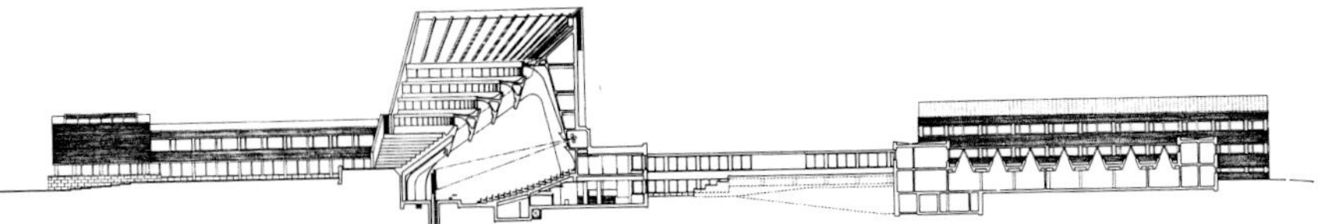

Fig. 80 Alvar Aalto, Otaniemi Institute of Technology, Otaniemi, Finland. 1949–64. Section.

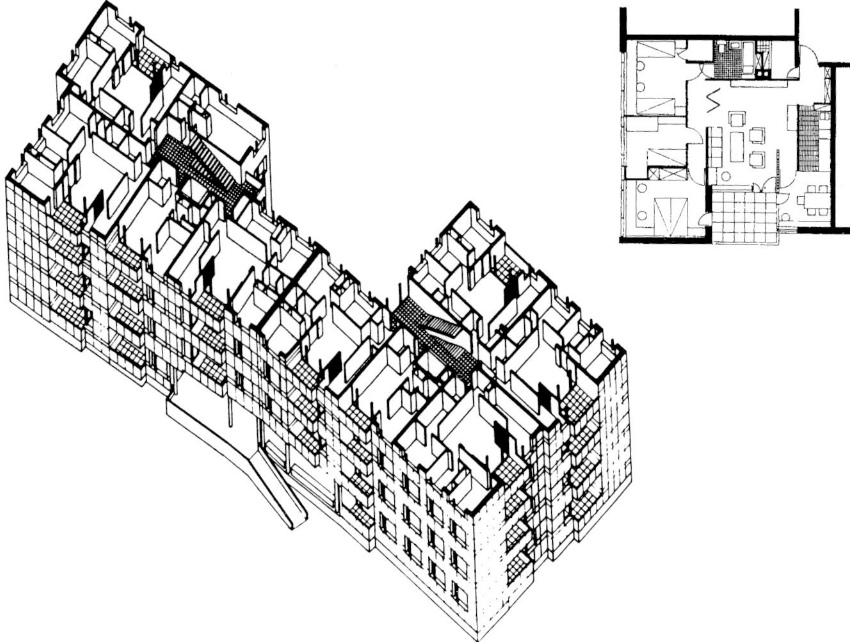

Fig. 81 Alvar Aalto, Hansaviertel Apartment Building, Berlin, Germany. 1957. Unit plan plus axonometric.

state socialism of the neighboring Soviet Union and the anarchic capitalism of the post-1945 Pax Americana. Of his anti-avant gardist, anti-mechanistic, heterotopic stance Aalto wrote in 1960:

> To make architecture more human means better architecture, and it means a functionalism much larger than the merely technical one. This goal can be accomplished only by architectural methods – by the creation and combination of different technical things in such a way that they will provide for the human being the most harmonious life. [22]

Aalto was never to demonstrate this principle more forcibly than in his Hansaviertel prototypical apartment block completed for the Berlin Interbau Exhibition in 1957 (Fig. 81). In this instance,

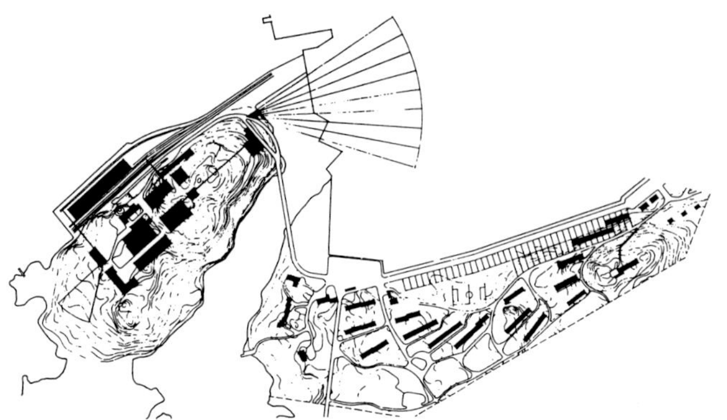

Fig. 82 Alvar Aalto, Sunila Factory & Workers' Housing, Sunila, Finland. 1935. Site plan.

each apartment is in effect a small single-story patio house, and the syncopated aggregation of which creates the semblance of a village on each floor. The basic unit is a three-bedroom apartment equipped with a bathroom and a kitchen grouped around three sides of a central living space that opens onto a generously proportioned terrace. Each terrace is shielded from the next and from the ground by virtue of the way it is incorporated into the block. A galley-kitchen gives direct access to this terrace for the purposes of eating outdoors, while the kitchen itself is accessed from a generously proportioned internal foyer. Acoustic and visual privacy is facilitated throughout by a pattern of circulation that serves the flanking bedrooms while being partially screened from the central living volume. This carefully modulated arrangement is matched by the generosity of the glazed elevator hall serving each apartment cluster. Unlike the arrangement adopted in most apartment buildings, it is a naturally lit and ventilated volume, rather than an hermetic corridor. In ergonomic terms, this is surely the most brilliant, *middle-class* apartment plan devised in the entire century (Fig. 82).

While Le Corbusier displayed comparable ingenuity in the development of high-rise dwelling units, from his Maison Clarté, Geneva of 1932 to his post-war Unité d'habitation, these were invariably either too Spartan to be popular or, alternatively, where luxurious, were too expensive to be made readily available to society at large. Hence, the fundamental limitations of his heroic Unité d'habitation realized in Marseilles in 1948–54, a building which, while fully occupied today, was perhaps never fully suited for working-class occupation, neither economically nor sociologically.

The advantages of Aalto's Hansaviertel prototype do not end with the units themselves however, for the modular rhythm of the block, established through its precast concrete, modular wall system, sets up a significant interplay with the inset terraces that are incorporated into its form. These terraces also play a rhythmic role at another scale in that the raised soffits above the living rooms impart a "noble" identity to each apartment. Furthermore, the gray concrete panels, cast from steel formwork, are rhythmically jointed, so as to create a coursed effect reminiscent of stone facing on a gigantic scale – the trace, one might say, of Aalto's Nordic Classical origins. At the same time, the partially protruding terraces, opening toward the south, impart an organic direction to the mass as this is determined by the sun.

It is important to note how the Hansaviertel block was partially derived from the equally prototypical low-rise, high-density workers' housing that Aalto designed for the Sunila pulp mill complex in 1935 (Fig. 83) and from his Kauttua terraced housing completed in 1940. In Sunila the low-rise blocks fan out across the site, splaying apart according to both the orientation and the fall of the land, whereas in Kautta they step down a slope, the roof of one apartment serving as the terrace for the apartment immediately above it. Like Ludwig Mies van der Rohe and Ludwig Hilberseimer, both of whom were subject to the influential ecological writings of Raoul Francé, Aalto envisaged a continual urbanization of the earth's surface, one in which his mythical "forest town", as opposed to the Anglo-Saxon garden city, would come to be universally adopted in northern Europe and perhaps even elsewhere as a kind of universal, ecological land-settlement pattern. Aalto justified his "forest-town" in terms that were reminiscent of the views advanced in

Fig. 83 The low-rise, high-density worker's housing, Aalto designed for the Sunila pulp mill complex, south facade. 1935.

Bruno Taut's *The Dissolution of Cities* of 1920. Thus, we find him writing of his 1940 regional plan for the Kokemäenjoki River Valley as follows:

> Exactly as the medieval cities once upon a time lost their fortification walls and the modern city grew out beyond them, the concept of the city today is in the process of shedding its constraints. But this time it is happening, not to lead once again to the creation of a larger unit, but rather so that the city will become part of the countryside, the underlying meaning of such regional plans is that they synchronize country and city.[23]

Despite their flexible character, Aalto's regional plans remained mostly unrealized due to land speculation and the bureaucratic tendency to favor the productive norms of repetitive high-rise prefabrication, rather than accept the more subtle, low-rise organic morphology favored by Aalto. These reactionary forces, prevalent even in the Finnish welfare state, did not inhibit the realization of Aalto's smaller civic complexes however, where a topographical approach enabled him to establish the identity of a place through the way in which the built form extended into the site. This is at once evident in the case of the Säynätsalo Town Hall which was conceived as the culmination of a series of structures running through the town center. Here Taut's "city crown" came to be recalled through the mono-pitched roof of the council chamber. A similar roof form appears in most of Aalto's civic centers with much the same intent, namely to serve as a symbolic core around which the rest of the settlement can develop.

Resisting closure around either a classical paradigm or a technological norm, Aalto strove for an organic flexibility, wherein function and production would play their respective roles without over-determining the form and where agriculture and industry would each interact with the landscape in such a way as to engender a symbiosis conducive to a broad range of human needs.

It is one of the ironies of the modern movement that while the deurbanizing principle of Aalto's forest town was directly inspired by the regional planning paradigms of the TVA and the Green Belt New Towns, realized in the United States in the 30s and the 40s, the full potential of these pioneering prototypes was ultimately demonstrated in Finland rather than in North America; above all in the "forest town" of Tapiola built outside Helsinki over the years 1949–62. The reasons for this are both political and circumstantial for where the social-democratic Finnish state was confronted with a major rebuilding program at the end of the war, the resurgent laissez-faire capitalism of the United States, triumphant after both winning the war and overcoming the Depression, began to sell its state-subsidized Green Belt New Towns back into private ownership, bringing the Roosevelt New Deal to a premature end.

Aalto may be seen as belonging to that group of Northern European architects who were concerned that building should be life-giving rather than repressive. This meant that the rigidity of any orthogonal grid should always be interrupted and inflected where the idiosyncrasies of either the site or the program demanded it. In 1960 Leonardo Benevolo summed up Aalto's mediation of technological modernization and rationality in the following way:

> In the first modern buildings the constancy of the right angle served mainly to generalize the compositional process of instituting a *priori* geometrical relationships between all the elements, which meant that all conflicts could be resolved geometrically, with the balancing of lines, surfaces and volumes. The use of the oblique [as in Aalto's Paimio Sanitarium of 1928–33] pointed the way towards a contrary process, that of making the forms more individual and precise, allowing imbalance and tension to exist and to be balanced by the physical consistency of the elements and surroundings. Such architecture lost in didactic rigour but gained in warmth, richness and feeling, and ultimately extended its field of action, because the process of individualization was based on the already recognized generalizing method and indeed presupposed it. [24]

Aalto's approach engendered a poetic yet accessible mode of building, one which not only continued the Finnish national tradition in modern terms but also exercised a wide influence outside Scandinavia on works as varied as Charles Moore's Sea Ranch complex built in Sonoma County, California in 1965 and James Stirling's dormitory building realized for the University of St Andrews in Scotland in 1968. Aalto's influence would also extend to Iberia, asserting itself as a formative presence on works as various as Fernando Alba's El Rollo monastery in Salamanca of 1962 and Alvaro Siza's Quinta da Conceicao swimming pool completed in Matosinhos, Portugal in 1965. In fact the work of Aalto will remain as a primary inspiration on Iberian architecture throughout the remainder of the century as we may judge from Rafael Moneo's Miró Foundation realized in Palma de Mallorca in 1992.

Part 3:

Universal Civilization and National Cultures 1935–1998

Opposed to the Regionalism of Restriction is another type of regionalism, the Regionalism of Liberation. This is the manifestation of a region that is especially in tune with the emerging thought of the time. We call such a manifestation "regional" only because it has not yet emerged elsewhere ... A region may develop ideas. A region may accept ideas. In California in the late Twenties and Thirties modern European ideas met a still-developing regionalism. In New England, on the other hand, European Modernism met a rigid and restrictive regionalism that at first resisted and then surrendered. New England accepted European Modernism whole because its own regionalism had been reduced to a collection of restrictions.
Harwell Hamilton Harris 1954 [25]

The phenomenon of universalization, while being an advancement of mankind, at the same time constitutes a sort of subtle destruction, not only of traditional cultures, which might not be an irreparable wrong, but also of what I shall call for the time being the creative nucleus of great cultures, that nucleus on the basis of which we interpret life, what I shall call in advance the ethical and mythical nucleus of mankind. The conflict springs up from there. We have the feeling that this single world civilization at the same time exerts a sort of attrition or wearing away at the expense of the cultural resources a sort of attrition or wearing away at the expense of the cultural resources which have made the great civilizations of the past. This threat is expressed, among other disturbing effects, by the spreading before our eyes of a mediocre civilization which is the absurd counterpart of what I was just calling elementary culture. Everywhere throughout the world, one finds the same bad movie, the same slot machines, the same plastic or aluminum atrocities, the same twisting of language by propaganda, etc. It seems as if mankind, by approaching *en masse* a basic consumer culture, were also stopped *en masse* at a subcultural level. Thus we come to the crucial problem confronting nations just rising from underdevelopment. In order to get on to the road toward modernization, is it necessary to jettison the old cultural past which has been the *raison d'être* of a nation? ... Whence the paradox: on the one hand, it has to root itself in the soil of its past, forge a national spirit, and unfurl this spiritual and cultural revindication before the colonialist's personality. But in order to take part in modern civilization. It is necessary at the same time to take part in scientific, technical and political rationality, something which very

often requires the pure and simple abandon of a whole cultural past. It is a fact: every culture cannot sustain and absorb the shock of modern civilization. There is the paradox: how to become modern and return to sources; how to revive an old , dormant civilization and take part in universal civilization.
Paul Ricoeur, History and Truth, 1961 [26]

3.1 Community and Society

The opposition between "community" and "society" with which this essay began, that is to say between societies based on traditional forms of rooted *culture* that are primarily agrarian in character and those that are subject to a hypothetically universal techno-scientific principle, largely based on Taylorized industrial production, sets the stage for the social-cultural polarity that assumes different forms throughout the 20th century, affecting every aspect of contemporary life and above all architecture.

This split between on the one hand universal civilization and on the other idiosyncratic tribal or national cultures (that aspect of culture that Paul Ricoeur would characterize as the ethical and mythical nuclei of mankind) seems to resurface in architecture in a particularly striking way after the initial triumph of the European *avant-garde* between the years 1918 to 1929. It is surely no accident that a naïve belief in the immediate realizability of the *modern project* (dating back to the French Enlightenment) would announce itself in architecture with remarkable energy and conviction between the end of the First World War (the mythical "war to end all wars") and the Great Crash of 1929 which disrupted the socio-economic equilibrium of the capitalist world throughout its length and breadth; engendering a crisis from which it would not recover, until the Second World War (1939–45) and its aftermath of reconstruction and renewed prosperity.

The major left-wing revolutions that attended the ideological thrust and counter-thrust of the modern project over this period (i.e. the Russian Bolshevik Revolution occurring effectively at the beginning of the epoch in October 1917 and the Chinese Communist Revolution, led by Mao Tse-Tung over the years 1934–48) may both be seen as the *active* context against which the *reactionary* Fascist revolutions of Europe and Asia came into being. As a result of these successive global disturbances it became increasingly clear that modernization, most frequently personified in architecture by the white, abstract rationality of the International Style, would not come into being overnight as a brave new world, but would instead be subject to an infinite series of reversals and deviations, not to mention the sporadic violent conflicts at both local and global scale that will be fought in its name.

With all the acuteness that is characteristic of the creative mind at its most sensitive, the so-called pioneers of the modern movement began in various ways to qualify the modern project, either by reinterpreting the vernacular in terms of modern technology in order to create an architecture that was socially more accessible and hence capable of embodying local values while still being engaged in modernization or, alternatively, reverting in some measure, to the stereometric regularity of classicism in order to represent the authority of the State, along with its corporate subsets and vestiges of traditional institutions. For the purposes of this condensed account these two impulses may be adumbrated in parallel, first in terms of the global influence of Le Corbusier as this permeated the so-called Third World, above all Latin America, Japan and India, and second in terms of the New Monumentality, prefigured as we have already seen in the work of the Italian Rationalists between 1926 and 1945 and inaugurated in more revisionist terms in the American movement known as the New Monumentality that surfaced with particular vigor after 1945 in the post-war work of Louis Kahn and Mies van der Rohe and in all the postmodern monumental structures that followed in their wake, erected in the name of the Pax Americana.

3.2 The Influence of Le Corbusier in England, Latin America and Japan: 1935–1970

The British 1987 centennial exhibition *Le Corbusier: Architect of the Century* more than adequately expressed the undeniable dominance of Le Corbusier's thought and work on the architecture in this century; an influence that was more global perhaps after the Second World War when, despite Bruno Zevi's proselytizing, the influence of Wright faded in favor of a *modus operandi* that was less idiosyncratic. The generic appeal of Le Corbusier was evident even before the war, particularly in England where surprisingly enough, given the strength of its native traditions, a Neo-Purist architecture became a discernible mode after the 1927 publication of *Vers une architecture* in English. The most accomplished exponent of this genre in Britain in the 30s was the Russian émigré architect Berthold Lubetkin (Tecton) whose Highpoint I apartment block built in London in 1935 helped to consolidate the British modern movement in the pre-war period. While the Second World War foreclosed on this movement in Europe, Le Corbusier in his post-Purist, "brutalist" mode was once again enthusiastically received as an influence in England in the 1950s. This is at once evident from Alison and Peter Smithson's Golden Lane Housing proposal of 1952 (Fig. 84) and Stirling and Gowan's *bêton brut*, brick faced flats completed near Richmond, Surrey in 1958. The so-called New Brutalism that thus emerged in England at this time was partially influenced by Le Corbusier's *brut* architecture. It was also equally informed by Alvar Aalto and Louis Kahn, as we may judge from Stirling and Gowan's Engineering Building built for Leicester University in 1959 (Fig. 85).

Fig. 84 Alison and Peter Smithson, Golden Lane Housing, London, England. 1952. Perspective.

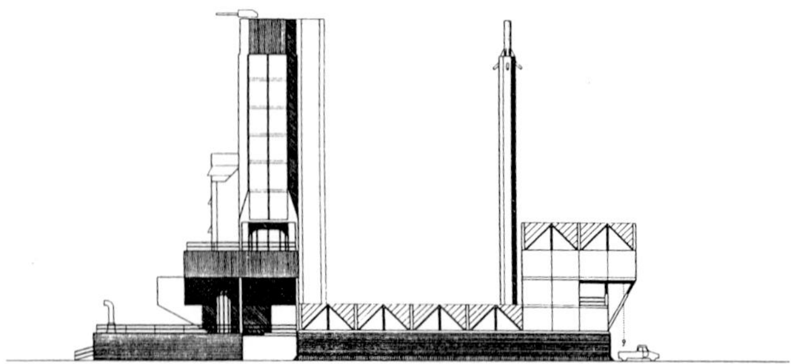

Fig. 85 Stirling and Gowan Engineering Faculty, University of Leicester, England. 1959.

Aside from his exceptional sensitivity and talent as a designer, Le Corbusier's prewar influence, particularly after the publication of the first volume of his complete works in 1930, stemmed in large measure from the typological character of his thought. More than any other architect of his generation he elaborated a modern building typology, applicable across a wide variety of uses. This penchant for the normative plus his invention of the free plan as the spatial corollary of the concrete frame enabled him to accommodate a wide spectrum of functions within a generic orthogonal volume. At the same time he was able to exploit the elementarist method of the Ecole des Beaux Arts so as to assemble larger complexes that were able to embody monumental civic institutions, as this was demonstrated at the end of his Purist period in his proposals for the League of Nations (1927) (Fig. 86) and the Palace of the Soviets (1931) (Fig. 87).

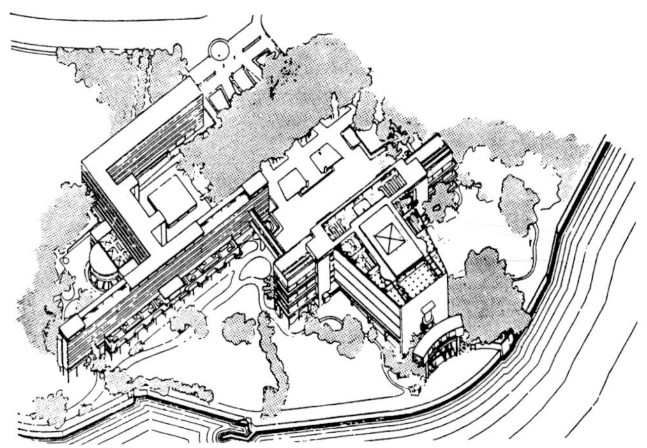

Fig. 86 Le Corbusier and Pierre Jeanneret, League of Nations competition, Geneva. 1927. Axonometric.

Fig. 87 Le Corbusier and Pierre Jeanneret, Palais des Soviets competition, Moscow. 1931. Perspective of forum.

His typological, elementarist method first proved its capacity for differentiated development in the modernization of Brazil during the second half of the 30s, most particularly after his second visit to Brazil in 1936 when he collaborated with a team of young architects, led by Lucio Costa, on a joint project for a building for the new Ministry of Education in Rio de Janeiro (Fig. 88). In this work, his "five-points", plus the *brises soleils* that he had first devised for use in North Africa, proved susceptible to regional inflection, particularly in the early work of Oscar Niemeyer, who played a salient role in the design of the ministry and then went on to develop his own free-form manner in his Brazilian Pavilion for the New York World Fair of 1939 (Fig. 89). In collaboration with the painter / landscape architect Roberto Burle-Marx, Niemeyer was able to augment the spatial potential of the free plan so as to extend its topographic continuity beyond the confines of the building. Thus Niemeyer transformed Le Corbusier's Purist syntax into a plasticity that was

Fig. 88 Le Corbusier, Lucio Costa and Oscar Niemeyer, Ministry of Education, Rio de Janeiro, Brazil. 1939.

Fig. 89 Oscar Niemeyer, Brazilian Pavilion, New York World's Fair. 1939. Perspective.

evocative of the Brazilian Baroque, while Burle-Marx enriched this expression through the equally organic deployment of exotic plant material, much of it having been found through botanical expeditions in the rainforests of the country.

Fig. 90 Oscar Niemeyer, Casino, Pampulha, Brazil. 1942.

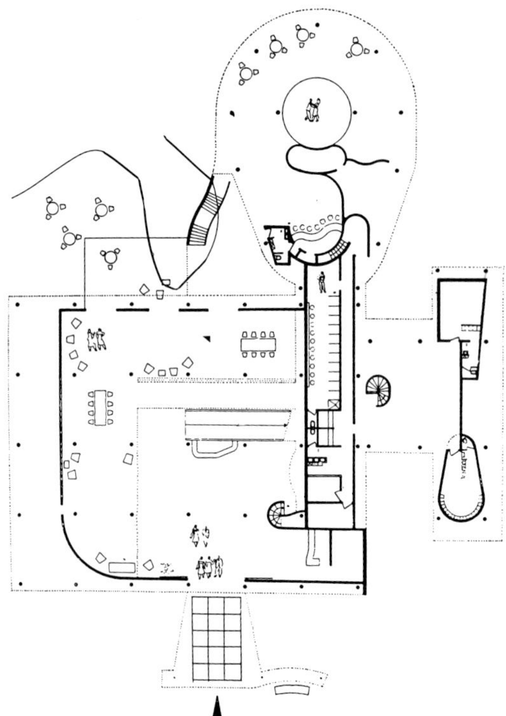
Fig. 91 Oscar Niemeyer, Casino, Pampulha, Brazil. 1942. Ground Floor Plan.

Niemeyer's genius matured in 1942 when he realized the casino at Pampulha, near Belo Horizonte. Here he reinterpreted the Corbusian notion of a *promenade architecturale* in a spatial composition of remarkable vivacity. This was a plastically expressive work in every respect, from the welcoming double-height foyer of the gleaming ramps rising to the gaming floor to the elliptical corridors giving onto the restaurant and the circular dance floor (Figs. 90 & 91). Hedonistic in its general treatment, the building displayed a strong contrast in mood between the propriety of its facades faced in travertine and juparana stone and the exoticism of its interior lined with pink glass, satin and traditional Portuguese tiles.

This building, plus a yacht club (Fig. 92), a shell concrete church and a lakeside dance pavilion, all built in Pampulha, demonstrated the full potential of Niemeyer's Brazilian modernism, that aside from representing a national ethos also encapsulated a liberative, spatial culture of unparalleled generosity. While Niemeyer later turned towards the New Monumentality in the governmental structures that he designed for the new capital of Brasilia in 1955, the brilliance of his initial vision was sufficient to inspire a discernibly Brazilian architecture that seems to have endured across half a century of practice, not only through the work of Niemeyer himself, but also in terms of many other talented Brazilian architects from Affonso Reidy and Rino Levi, to Lina Bo Bardi and Paulo Mendes da Rocha. This last figure is possibly the leading architect of the succeeding generation to Niemeyer as we may judge from his remarkable Paulistan Athletic Club completed in São Paulo

Fig. 92 Oscar Niemeyer, Yacht Club, Pampulha, Minas Gerais, Brazil. 1942.

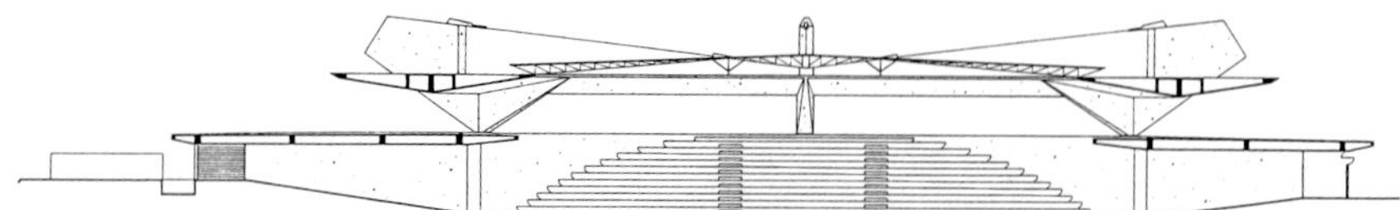

Fig. 93 Paulo Mendes da Rocha, Paulistino Athletics Club Gymnasium, São Paulo, Brazil. 1957–61.

in 1961 (Fig. 93). Once again we seem to encounter that characteristically simple yet structurally daring and spatially generous use of monolithic reinforced concrete construction that is characteristically Brazilian.

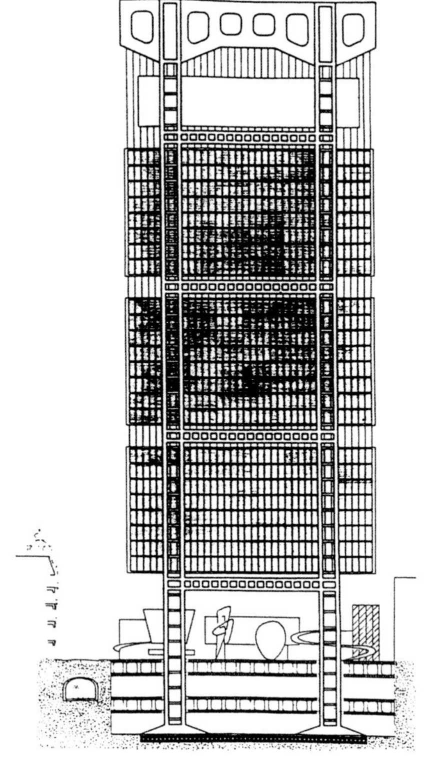

Fig. 94 Amancio Williams, Skyscraper Project. 1946–48. Elevation and section.

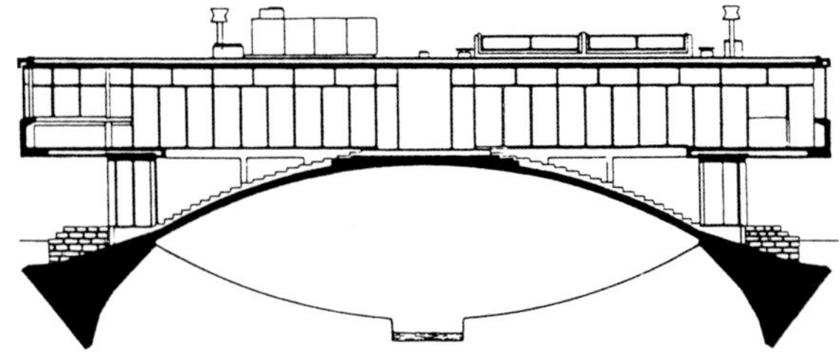

Fig. 95 Amancio Williams, Williams House, Mar del Plata, Argentina. 1945. Section.

Apart from Le Corbusier's catalytic impact on Brazil, contemporary architecture in Latin America is virtually unimaginable without the Corbusian point of departure that established the ground, so to speak, for opening up the plastically expressive potential of reinforced concrete construction in all its aspects. The largely unrealized work of the Argentine architect Amancio Williams is a case in point, who after serving as site architect for Le Corbusier's Curuchet House in La Plata (1949) will surpass the plastic potential of Le Corbusier's Purist architecture in a series of brilliant proposals for experimental concrete structures, conceived over the period 1954–68. These range from shell concrete canopies carried on mushroom columns to high-rise exoskeleton structures the floors of which were projected as being cable suspended from heavy concrete trusses at the crown of the building (Fig. 94). Williams' bridge house for his father in Mar del Plata (1945) (Fig. 95) modeled on Robert Maillart's paradigmatic concrete bridges will point in much the same direction. Some of these suggestions will be eventually developed by others, most notably perhaps by the Argentine Clorindo Testa in his extraordinary concrete exoskeleton structure for the Bank of London and South America completed in Buenos Aires in 1959 (Fig. 96). In fact the case may be made that Williams influenced successive generations of Argentine architects, causing

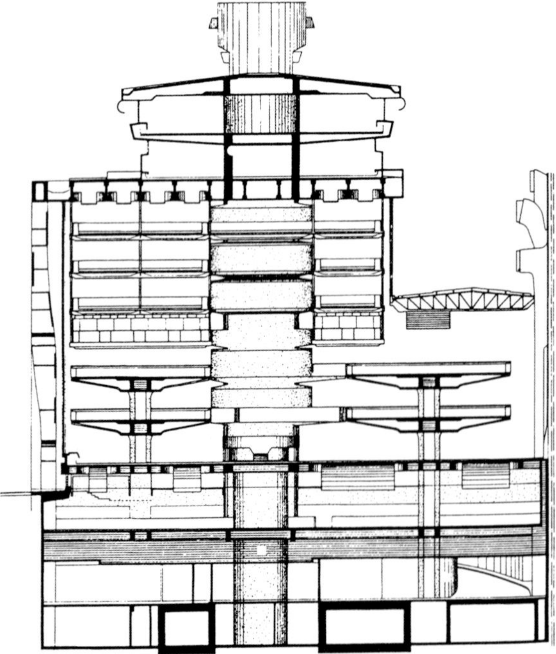

Fig. 96 Clorindo Testa, Bank of London and South America, Buenos Aires, Argentina 1959–66. Section.

them to develop their practices in an equally bold tectonic direction, above all the co-operative practice of Manteola, Sanchez, Gomez, Santos, Solsona and Viñoly, who between 1969 and 1978 produced a series of structurally rationalist modern buildings including the masterly BCBA branch bank building erected in the Retiro district of Buenos Aires in 1969 (Figs. 97 & 98). One of a series of glass block banks built for the Banco de la Ciudad de Buenos Aires this concrete

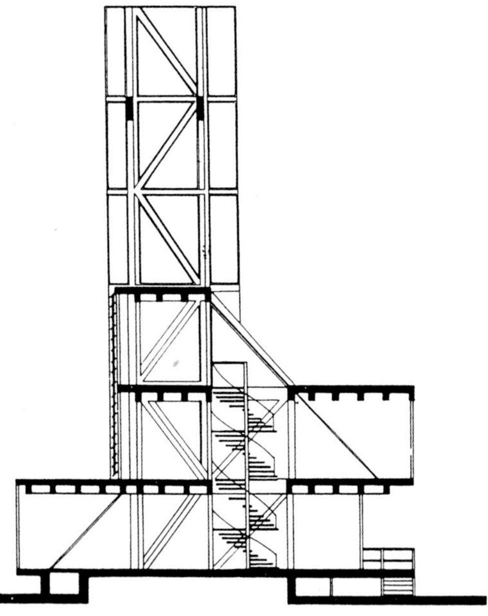

Fig. 97 Manteola, Sanchez, Gomez, Santos, Solsona and Vinoly et al, BCBA Branch Bank, Retiro, Argentina. 1969. Section.

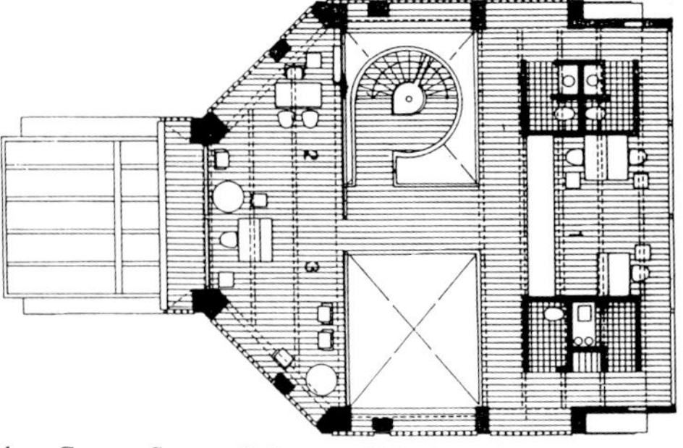

Fig. 98 Manteola, Sanchez, Gomez, Santos, Solsona and Vinoly et al, BCBA Branch Bank, Retiro, Argentina. 1969. Plan.

framed, tower-like diminutive structure displayed a neo-constructivist syntax taken in part from Testa's canonical bank building and in part from Stirling's engineering faculty for Leicester University.

As the demi-urge of the century, Le Corbusier's influence extended well beyond the confines of Europe and Latin America to serve as a point of departure for an inflected modern architecture in Japan and South Asia. As in the case of Brazil, the influence will be carried forward by certain key figures; in Japan Junzo Sakakura and Kunio Mayekawa and in India by Balkrishna Doshi, all three having worked for Le Corbusier in Paris during their early careers; Sakakura and Mayekawa in the 30s, prior to the Second World War, and Doshi in the immediate post-war period, most particularly as job captain on the monumental complex that Le Corbusier designed for Chandigarh, which was not only destined to become the new capital of the Punjab but also the symbolic centerpiece for Jawaharlal Nehru's plan for the modernization of India.

Where Doshi will eventually derive his expression as much from the American architect Louis Kahn as from Le Corbusier-drawing on this later influence in order to move away from the Corbusian obsession with concrete, and thus to re-validate brick as we find this in his own house built in Ahmedabad in 1961-Sakakura will turn towards steel for the framing of his Japanese pavilion built for the Paris World exhibition of 1937 (Fig. 99) and for his post-war Kamakura Museum of Modern Art of 1951. (Fig. 100) He seems to have been motivated, in both instances, by the fact

Fig. 99 Junzo Sakakura, Japanese Pavilion, World Exhibition, Paris, France. 1937. Axonometric.

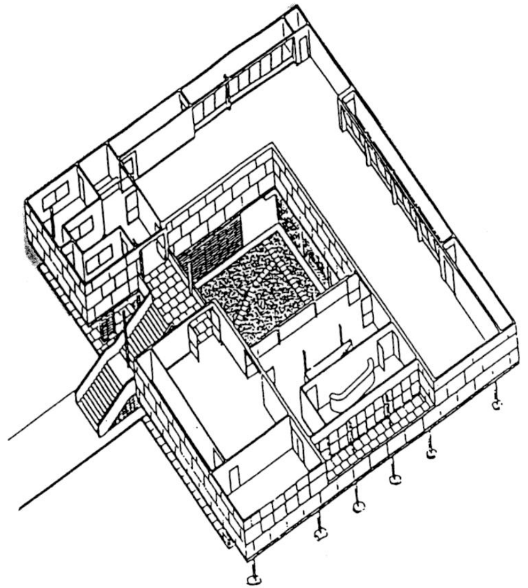

Fig. 100 Junzo Sakakura, Kamakura Museum of Art, Japan. 1951. Axonometric.

that steel framing could be seen as lying closer to the timber vernacular of Japan. Be this as it may, fire-proof, reinforced concrete construction was already well established as a standard practice in Japan, long before Sakakura's return from Paris and it was to become the anti-seismic method par excellence during the second decade of the century, leading to such proto-modern pieces as Antonin Raymond's monolithic concrete town house, realized in Tokyo in 1923. While the Czech-American Raymond had not worked for Le Corbusier, his contribution to the development of a Neo-Corbusian, reinforced concrete syntax in Japan was seminal, in part no doubt because his most talented Japanese assistant in the 1930s was Mayekawa, who had been apprenticed to Le Corbusier prior to working for Raymond in 1932.

Apart from the Neo-Corbusian work of Raymond and Mayekawa one should also note that the Japanese modern movement was initially inspired in the 20s by German Expressionism, that is to say the organic Bunri Ha movement, before its turn towards the functionalism of the Neue Sachlichkeit at the end of the decade as we find this in Sutemi Horiguchi's metereological station built on the island of Oshima in 1928. Thus while Mayekawa's unrealized competition entries for the Ueno Museum, Tokyo (1931) and for the Mutual Life Insurance Co (1933) will echo the latent monumentality of Le Corbusier's League of Nations design of 1927, Neo-Corbusianism will not fully establish itself in Japan until the 50s, above all through the seminal role played by Mayekawa's pupil Kenzo Tange, first with Tange's Hiroshima Peace Park and Atomic Memorial Museum (1955), built close to the epicenter of the first atomic bomb and then in Tange's brilliant Tokyo Bay Plan of 1960 (Fig. 101) and his Kagawa Prefectural Office, Takamatsu of 1958 (Fig. 102). Where the former was patently a megastructural "orientalization" of the generic ideas underlying Le Corbusier's Radiant City project of 1934, the Kagawa Prefecture was able to translate the boldness of Le Corbusier's post-war concrete syntax into a *bêton brut* version of the Daibutsu wooden style of the 12th century as we find this in the Todaiji precinct at Nara, which for Tange embodied the essence of Japanese national culture. But this was by no means the end of Tange's reactive relationship with Le Corbusier, whose Philips Pavilion of 1958 (Fig. 103) would find a dramatic echo in Tange's Totsuka Country Clubhouse of 1961 and even more directly in his spectacular National Olympic Stadium, Tokyo of 1964 (Figs. 104 & 105).

Mayekawa was equally influenced by the postwar work of Le Corbusier. This is most apparent in Mayekawa's Harumi Apartments, Tokyo (1956) (Figs. 106 & 107), which were partially modeled on Le Corbusier's Unité d'habitation, Marseilles of 1952. The Harumi slab block was a hybrid work that sought to assimilate Western paradigms into the Japanese tradition and vice versa. This it did in part by furnishing the interior of its heavy, anti-seismic concrete frame with traditional Japanese timber-framed linings, equipped with sliding partitions and *tatami* matting throughout. That this juxtaposition could at best only mediate the cultural upheaval induced by

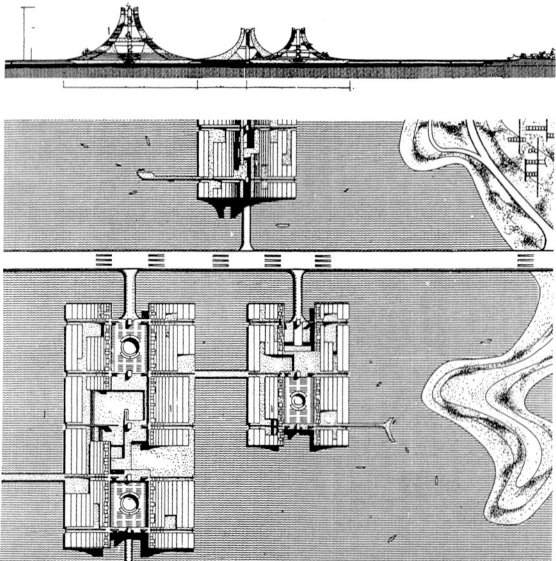

Fig. 101 Kenzo Tange, Tokyo Bay Plan, Tokyo, Japan, 1960.

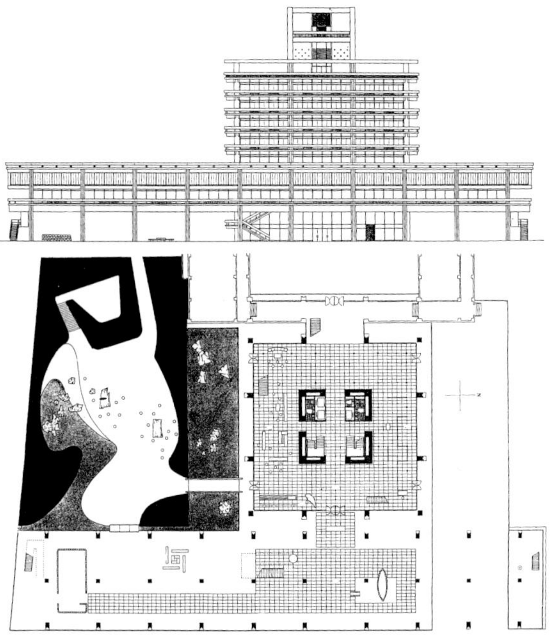

Fig. 102 Kenzo Tange, Kagawa Prefecture, Takamatsu, Japan. 1955–58. Elevation and plan.

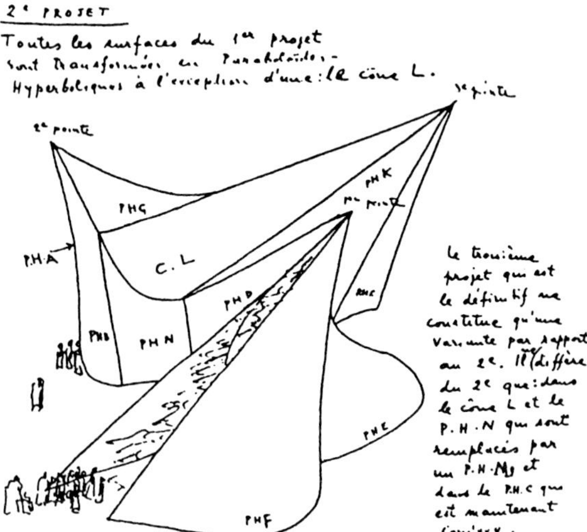

Fig. 103 Le Corbusier, Phillips Pavilion, Brussels World Fair, 1958.

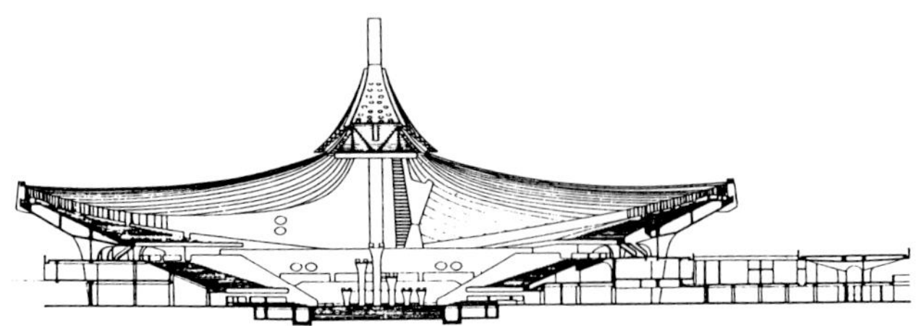

Fig. 104 Kenzo Tange, Yoyogi Olympic Stadium, Shibuyiku, Tokyo, Japan 1961–64. Roof section.

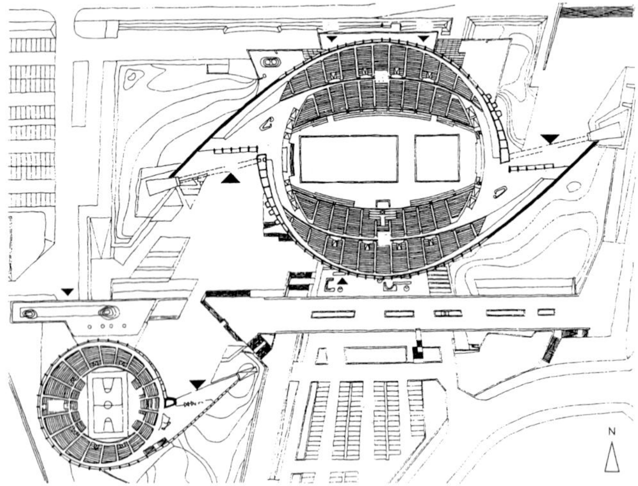

Fig. 105 Kenzo Tange, Yoyogi Olympic Stadium, Shibuyiku, Tokyo, Japan 1961–64. Site plan.

modernization was later recognized by Mayekawa when, like the Frankfurt School philosopher Herbert Marcuse, he felt obliged to acknowledge that techno-scientific modernization may not eventually have a beneficial outcome for the life of the species. Thus we find him writing in 1965:

> Modern architecture is and must be squarely based on the solid achievements of modern science, technology and engineering. Why then does it often tend to become something inhuman? I believe that one of the main reasons is that it is not always created merely to satisfy human requirements, but rather for some other reason, such as the profit motive. Or an attempt is made to cramp the architecture into the framework of some budget formulated by the mechanical operations of a powerful bureaucratic system of the modern state, this budget having nothing to do with human considerations. Another possibility is that inhuman elements may be contained within science, technology and engineer-

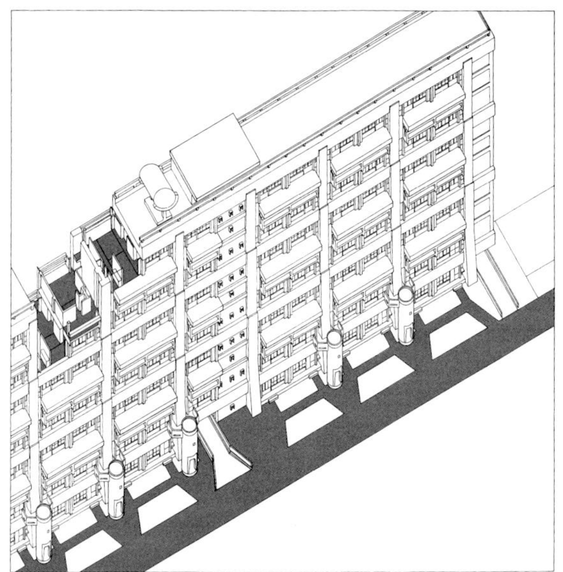

Fig. 106 Kunio Mayekawa, Harumi Apartments, Tokyo, Japan. 1956. Axonometric.

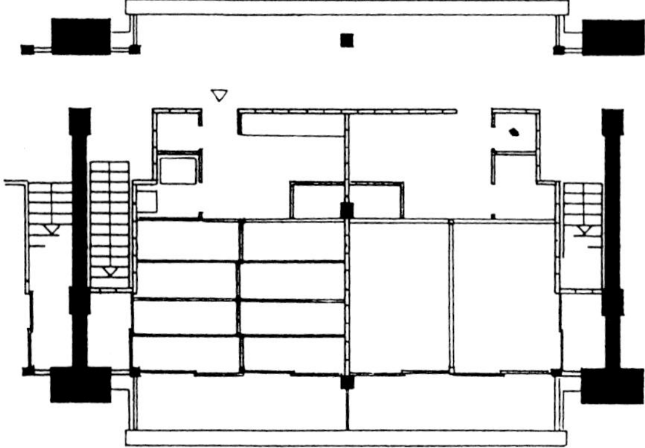

Fig. 107 Kunio Mayekawa, Harumi Apartments, Tokyo, Japan. 1956. Typical apartment plan with gallery access.

ing themselves. When man attempts to understand a certain phenomenon, the methods adopted are those of simplification and abstraction. The question arises of whether the use of such methods may not cause a departure from human realities ...
Modern architecture must recall its rudiments, its initial principles as a human architecture. Whereas science and engineering are the products of human brains, the modern archi-

tecture and the modern cities which are built by them tend to become inhuman. That which has beclouded the rudimentary principles of modern architecture, that which is distorting its sense of mission is today's ethical system of value judgements concealed behind this ethical system. These ethical and value criteria are forces which are moving modern civilization but are also obliterating human dignity and making a mockery of the Declaration of Human Rights. The conclusion of the tragedy is by no means simple. We must go back to the beginnings of Western civilization and discover whether the power to bring about such an ethical revolution can really be found in the inventory of Western civilization itself. If not, then we must seek it, together with Toynbee, in the Orient, or perhaps in Japan.
Kunio Mayekawa, *Thoughts on Civilization in Architecture*, 1965 [27]

Tange's reputation as an architect of world stature peaked during the 1960s as his practice took on an increasingly megastructural aspect from his Yamanashi Press and Broadcasting Center, Kofu (1966) (Fig. 108) to his plan for re-building Skopje, after the seismic disaster in the same year and his proposal to construct megastructural office buildings, spanning between tower supports, for the Tsukiji district of Tokyo (1967). All of these works were designed by the multidisciplinary URTEC team, an association of architects, engineers and planners that had been founded by Tange in 1961. However, Tange's heroic Neo-Corbusianism was about to lose its conviction as is suggested by the dematerialized space-frame of his Festival Plaza performance space, designed with Arata Isozaki for the Expo'70 in Osaka. Aside from the short-lived radical Metabolist movement (1959–64) led by the architectural critic Noboru Kawazoe, the next decade in Japan was dominated by the so-called Japanese New Wave that ushered such rising latter-day modernists as Fumihiko Maki, Toyo Ito and Tadao Ando, whose various expressions announced a fundamental break with the positivism of the Neo-Corbusian project. This rupture also caused architects like

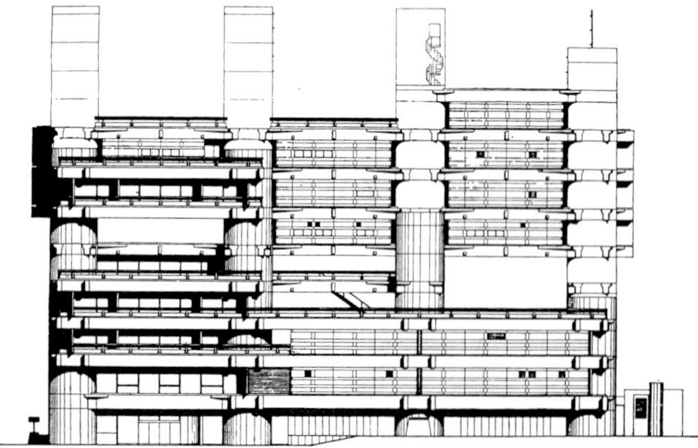

Fig. 108 Kenzo Tange, Yamanashi Broadcasting Center, Yamanashi, Kofu, Japan. 1961–66. Elevation.

Maki and Masato Ohtaka to move away from CIAM master-planning, to advocate instead the fragmentary aggregation of urban form, just as Ito and Ando in the mid-70s would withdraw within a "resistant" introspective domestic domain, as we find this in the courtyard houses that they both realized during this period.

3.3 The New Monumentality and the Pax Americana: 1943–1972

The founding intellectuals of the modern movement – namely the doyens of CIAM – were first compelled to come to terms with the problem of cultural identity and the need for representational form in the midst of the Second World War. The recognition that the avant-gardist modern project had failed in part through its social inaccessibility led them to confront the symbolic shortfall of the functionalist ethos in architecture, particularly as this had been formulated in the inter-war years by the International Constructivists. This reaction accounts, in large measure, for the manifesto "Nine Points on Monumentality" written while in exile in the United States by Sigfried Giedion, José Luis Sert and Fernand Léger in 1943. These nine points all pointed in various ways to the same fundamental concern, namely, the need for monumental buildings and equally representative public spaces to serve as collective symbols, whereby society could recognize its common identity and thus realize its destiny through the democratic consummation of both the monument and the place-form.

The reception of this critical *parti pris* in the United States was virtually instantaneous, taking the form of a conference organized around the theme of the New Monumentality in 1944 by the émigré scholar Paul Zucker; an event that seems to have been seminal to the evolution of American architecture in the post-war period, prompting, among other developments, the then unknown Philadelphia architect Louis Kahn to write his first theoretical text that addressed the theme of monumentality. Strangely enough, given the institutional emphasis of Giedion's "nine points," Kahn would argue that the monumentality of a given work depended upon its tectonic syntax rather than on its programmatic or typological substance.

While Kahn would eventually modify this materialistic stance, it is significant that his 1944 essay would stress the modernization of contemporary building practice and the new productive processes involved therein, rather than allude to the type or place-form that might be achieved through such procedures. It is even more ironic, given the ultimate evolution of his career, that Kahn's primary emphasis in 1944 was on the dematerializing capacity of space frames, fabricated out of welded tubular steel and clad entirely in glass (Fig. 109). In other words, subject to the influence of the American technocrat Richard Buckminster Fuller, Kahn would initially aspire to the paradox of an immaterial monumentality such as would come to be pursued from the early

70s onwards by such European Hi-Tech architects as Renzo Piano, Richard Rogers and Norman Foster.

Kahn's first and most significant attempt at combining tetrahedral space frame construction with monumental form came with his Yale Art Gallery of 1952 (Fig. 110), which in its articulation of servant and served spaces already suggests the influence of Frank Lloyd Wright's Larkin Building of 1906, particularly given the fact that Wright's office building had also been subdivided into servant and served spaces. This hierarchical separation in the Yale Art Gallery is given a certain expression through the diagrid reinforced concrete floors that span clear over the gallery volumes, ostensibly as space frames, even though they were eventually made from in situ concrete. Here we encounter for the first time Kahn's distinction between the honorific / monumental character of the galleries, roofed with diagrid floors, and the attendant "servant" spaces, escape stairs, lifts, lavatories, etc, roofed with flat slab construction.

The debt to the Larkin Building would become even more pronounced in Kahn's Richards Laboratories built at the University of Pennsylvania in 1959 (Figs. 111 & 112) where the blank, brick-

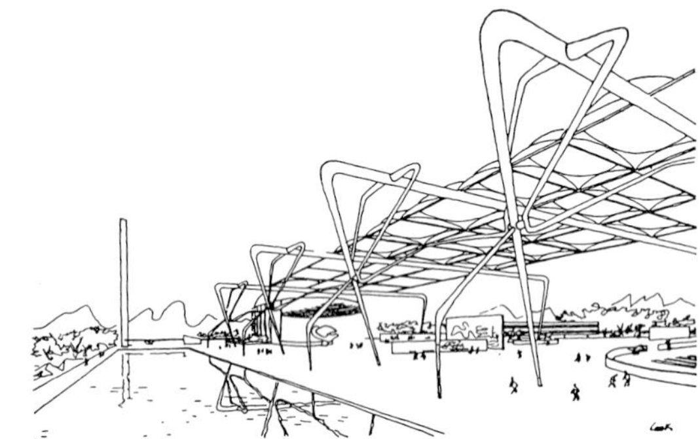

Fig. 109 Louis Kahn, Space Frame Exhibition Project. 1944.

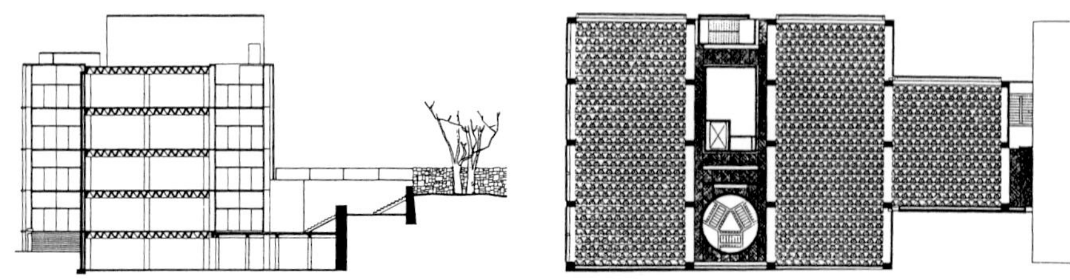

Fig. 110 Louis Kahn, Yale Art Gallery, New Haven, USA. 1952. Section and inverted ceiling plan.

Fig. 111 Louis Kahn, Richards Laboratories, University of Pennsylvania, Philadelphia, USA. 1959. Sketch of penultimate project.

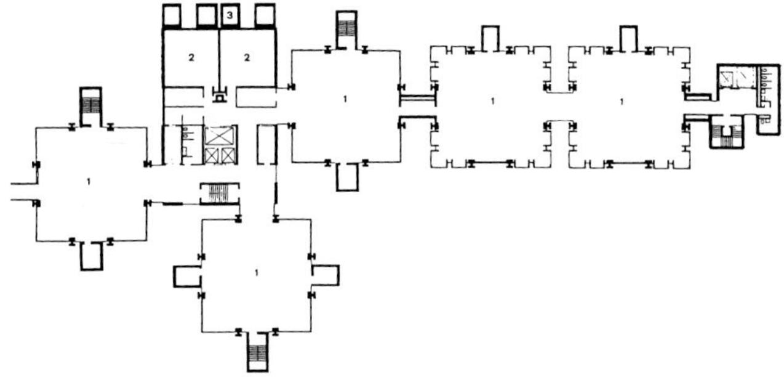

Fig. 112 Louis Kahn, Richards Laboratories, University of Pennsylvania, Philadelphia, USA. 1959. Plan.

encased "servant" shafts containing escape stairs and exhaust flues flank the laboratory clusters in such a way as to recall the corner stair towers and service shafts of the Larkin building that, as it happened, was demolished in the very year of its completion. Constructed out of post-tensioned, pre-cast concrete components, the "nine square" orthogonal space-frame floors of the laboratories themselves were rendered expressly without false ceilings as monumental space-forms, that given the eminently processal character of scientific experimentation, was somewhat willfully conceived by Kahn as honorific. For Kahn, all creativity, whether scientific or artistic, was seen as being divine and hence worthy of monumental treatment. This perhaps explains why his most successful buildings were either churches or their contemporary secular equivalents, namely, art museums, of which the Kimbell Art Museum realized in Fort Worth, Texas in 1972 was the most sublime work of his entire career (Figs. 113 & 114).

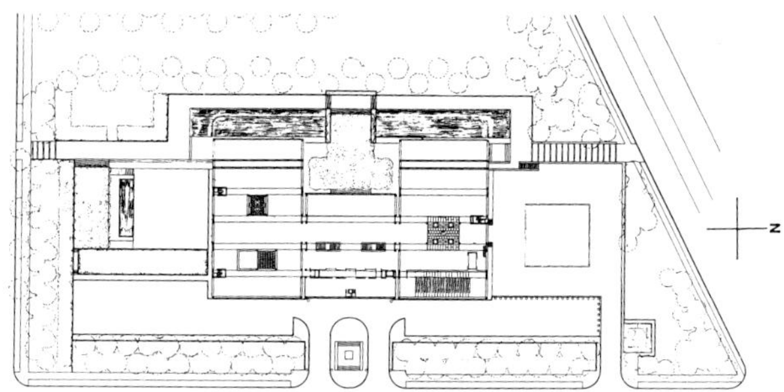

Fig. 113 Louis Kahn,Kimbell Museum, Fort Worth, Texas, USA. 1972. Site plan.

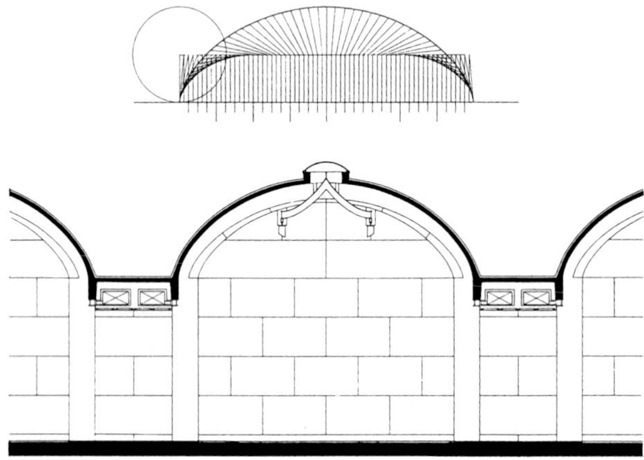

Fig. 114 Louis Kahn,Kimbell Museum, Fort Worth, Texas, USA. 1972. Detailed cross section with cycloid vault geometry.

In Kimbell, the space frame preoccupation is relinquished in favor of post-tensioned, long-span folded slab construction in concrete, which is the essential tectonic element out of which the museum is constituted. Here the dialectical interplay between modernization and monumentality comes to be explicitly articulated on many levels at once. In the first instance there are the distinctly different views as to what constitutes the most appropriate space for the exhibition of contemporary art; the open-planned, flexible loft space, or the traditional enfilade of top-lit rooms as we find this say in James Stirling's Staatsgalerie, Stuttgart of 1983. While Kahn opted for the former in his Yale Art Gallery of 1952, twenty years later when designing the Kimbell he would attempt a hybrid spatial form combining both modes at once, that is to say he would provide *discrete rooms* on the axis of the vaults that span clear as folded slabs over the 104 feet length of each gallery and, at the same time, *loft space*, running transversely, as it were, under these long spans. The opposition between these two contrasting axes of approach was ingeniously mediated by free-standing, full-height exhibition screens that were capable of being read as integral elements from either direction. The tension between modernization and monumentality arises at one other significant level in this work, namely the problem of access posed by universal car ownership since, in the case of the Kimbell Museum, only 15 per cent of the visitors enter via the honorific approach from the park. The remainder approach via the car park to the rear of the building and thus enter the museum by a stairway ascending to the central foyer. This contradiction echoes the even more generic and intrinsic conflict between automobile usage and civic form that Kahn tried to resolve without success in his various plans for the center of Philadelphia.

The extent to which Kahn's architecture was peculiar to the mores of the United States is perhaps insufficiently recognized, although this becomes patently evident once one acknowledges not only the influence of Wright on Kahn but also the seminal role played by the Ecole des Beaux Arts in North American architectural culture, exercising, as it did, not only an influence on Kahn who was trained under its aegis but also, in the last analysis, on Wright himself. In fact we have to recognize that the Ecole des Beaux Arts enabled the American architectural profession to emerge fully equipped at the end of the 19th century, to create virtually overnight all the monumental institutions that were required for the exploitation and organization of a vast continent during the first three decades of the century. We must also acknowledge that Kahn's penchant for building in brick devolved in large measure not only on its practicality but also on the prestige accorded to this material in New England from the foundation of the colonies onwards. While Kahn's architecture was not always an adequate response to the nuances of the American climate (a weakness it shared with the Neoclassicism of the Ecole) it is nonetheless clear that his application of shingles to the Salk Institute in San Diego was some kind of "regional" gesture, however much this particular form of cladding may have been transposed from the East coast of the States. On balance Kahn was too much of a formalist to be consistently responsive to the exigencies of climate as we may judge from the bizarre window openings applied to the government center in Dhaka which while they served to mitigate glare were rather unsuitable as far as cross-ventilation was concerned.

3.4 The influence of Louis Kahn in South Asia, Canada, Switzerland and Germany

Le Corbusier's influence had a different outcome from that of Kahn in South Asia for while his *bêton brut* manner served as an inspiring potential model for a modern, postcolonial architecture, particularly after the realization of his monumental works in Ahmedabad and Chandigarh in the 50s, his influence was soon to be overlaid by Kahn's structurally modular monolithic brick architecture which seems to have presented South Asian architects with an opportunity to re-discover

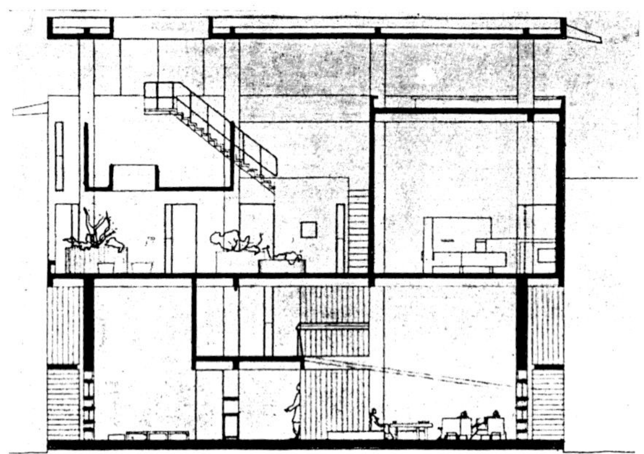

Fig. 115 Le Corbusier, Shodan House, Ahmedabad, India. 1952–56. Section.

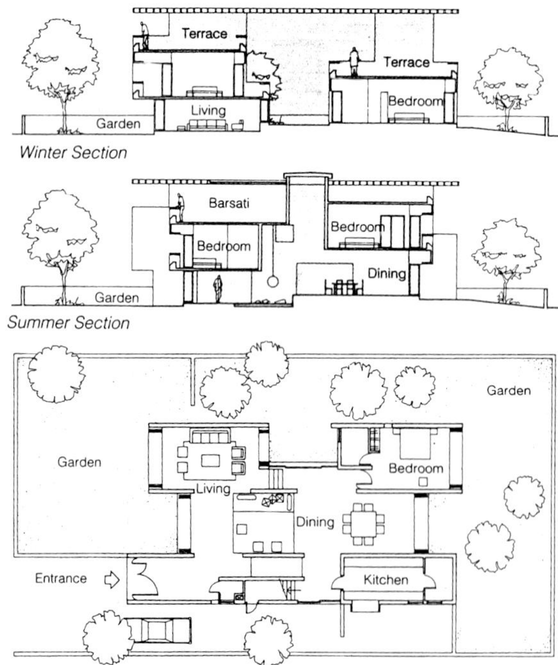

Fig. 116 Charles Correa, Parek House, Ahmedabad, India. 1968. Plan and section.

their own masonry traditions. Thus it is possible to witness South Asian variations in brick on the Corbusian concrete paradigm in three different houses that were each derived from Le Corbusier's Shodan House realized in Ahmedabad in 1956 (Fig. 115); Achyut Kanvinde's Harivallabas House of 1964, Charles Correa's Parek House of 1968, (Fig. 116) both built in Ahmedabad, and, lastly, Muzharul Islam's house completed in Dhaka, Bangladesh for his own occupation in 1969.

Apart from this Correa was perhaps at his most Corbusian in his so-called tube housing designed for the Gujarat Housing Board in 1962, where Le Corbusier's megaron type was manipulated in section so as to induce natural ventilation through the roof of the dwelling (Fig. 117). At the same time he will shift to a Neo-Kahnian approach for his Gandhi Memorial Museum realized in the Sabarmati Ashram, Ahmedabad in 1963; a work that derived, in some measure, from Kahn's Trenton Community Centre project of 1954. In a similar way, despite the fact that he had studied with Walter Gropius at Harvard (1942–47), Kahn's differentiation between *served* and *servant* space will become a recurrent theme in Kanvinde's architecture as is evident from his National Dairy Plant, Mehsana, Gujarat (1970–73) and his Nehru Science Centre, Bombay (1978–80) (Fig. 118), where ventilation shafts, recalling Kahn's Richards Laboratories, create a turreted architecture that simultaneously alludes to the Mughal tradition.

As we have already noted, Balkrishna Doshi worked with Le Corbusier on the design of Chandigarh throughout the first half of the 50s, returning to India to oversee the construction of the Capitol in 1955. Setting up his own office a year later, his first work of consequence was the Neo-Corbusian

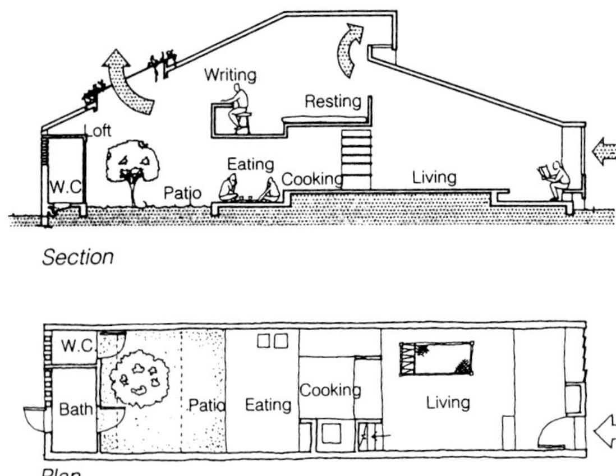

Fig. 117 Charles Correa, Tube House, Gujarat Housing Board. 1962.

Fig. 118 Achyut Kanvinde, Nehru Science Centre, Bombay, India. 1978–80. Perspective.

Institute of Indology (1962) but his own architecture changes decisively after he invites Kahn to India in 1962 to work on the Indian Institute Management in Ahmedabad (1962–74). In that year Doshi founds the Centre for Environmental Planning and Technology in Ahmedabad, serving as its first director and designing the foundation building in 1968; a structure that will mix Kahnian and Corbusian tropes with motifs taken from the Mughal tradition, particularly as this is to be found in Akbar's Fatehpur Sikri.

Indian architects will make a particularly accomplished "structuralist" contribution to the development of low-rise, high-density housing from the mid-60s onwards, starting with Raj Rewal's housing for the French Embassy in New Delhi (1967–69) and Doshi's housing for the Ecil Township, Hyderabad (1969–71). In effect this becomes a national movement that even today is still insufficiently recognized for its remarkable achievements from Doshi's Vidyahar Nagar and Aranya Townships of the period 1981–86 (Figs. 119 & 120), still under realization, to Raj Rewal's Sheikh Sarai Housing for New Delhi of 1980 (Fig. 121) and his more renowned sandstone-clad Olympic Village, realized for the same city of 1982. The Stein, Doshi and Balla office – the so called Sangat "think tank" – became a center for applied research in this area, producing a series of low-rise. low-cost housing projects, many of which have since been realized from the GSFC Township in Baroda (1964) to the LIC township in Hyderabad (1973). Much of this work has involved devising ways in which a simple, low cost dwelling may grow over time.

Charles Correa also made a series of seminal contributions to the theme of low-rise, high-density housing, above all in his prototypical Previ units built for a demonstration, international low-rise housing development realized in Lima, Peru in 1973. Around the same time, he collaborated with Pravina Mehta to design an exemplary exercise in high-rise housing at the other end of the social scale; his 28-story Kanchanjunga Apartment Tower for Bombay (1970–83), comprising 32

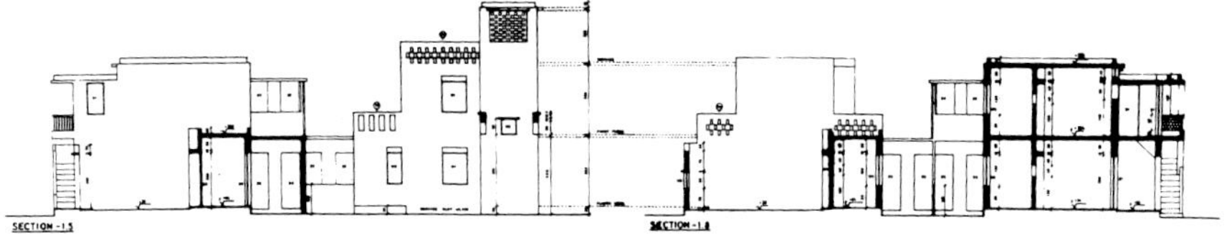

Fig. 119 Balkrishna Doshi, Aranya housing, Aranya Township, India. 1981–86. Sections.

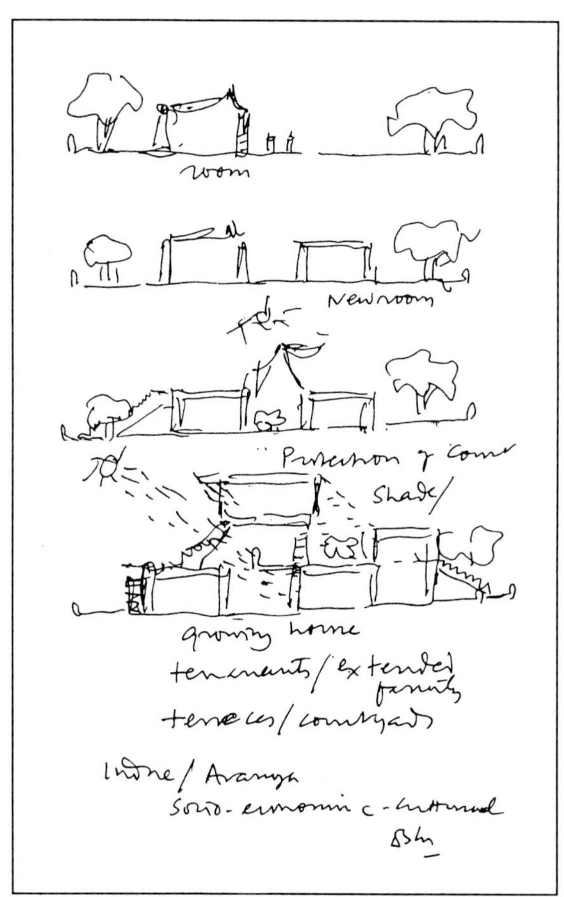

Fig. 120 Balkrishna Doshi, sketch exploring the possibilities for incremental growth, Aranya Township. 1981.

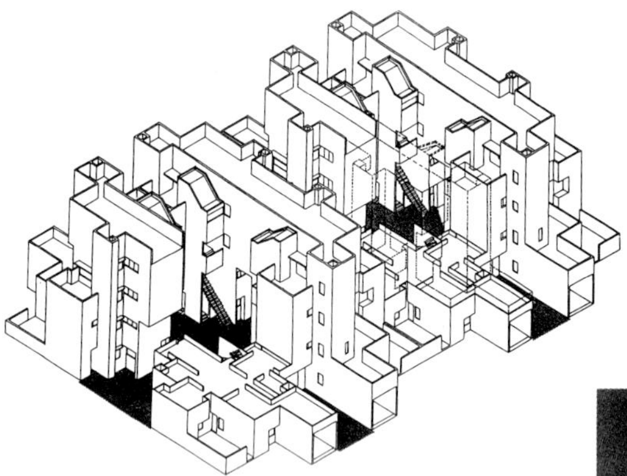

Fig. 121 Raj Rewal, Sheikh Sarai Housing, New Delhi, India. 1980. Axonometric.

Fig. 122 Charles Correa and Pravina Mehta, Kanchenjunga Apartments, Bombay, India. 1970–83.

interlocking duplexes ranging from 3 to 6 bedrooms in size (Fig. 122). In this singular work Correa combined the hanging garden concept embodied in Le Corbusier's Immeubles Villas of 1922 with more plastic, sectional episodes taken from the Marseilles Unité of 1952 and from his own equally Neo-Corbusian Tube House of a decade later. Here although the two-story garden terraces are covered by the units above, we have a move towards Correa's polemical emphasis on "open-to-sky space" which he considers to be the one rudimentary principle that has to be adhered to when building in the Indian socio-climatic context, irrespective of whether one is addressing low-cost housing or monumental public institutions. These last, invariably structured in Correa's work as low-rise labyrinths comprising enclosed courts and stepped terraces, assume a particularly felicitous form in his cultural buildings, ranging from his National Crafts Museum, New Delhi (1975–90) to his Jawahar Kala Kendra Cultural Centre, Jaipur (1986–92). This later work, dedicated to the memory of Nehru and clad on its exterior in red Agra sandstone, is a nine-square mandala in plan, ultimately deriving from the nine planets upon which the plan of Jaipur is said to have been based. This relatively simple single-story masonry structure grouped about a central, stepped *kund*, open to the sky, parallels the introspective patio type as this was adopted by leading Mexican architects from the early-60s onwards, above all by Luis Barragán and Ricardo Legorreta.

Within the spectrum of Neo-Kahnian architecture in the South Asian continent, Muzharul Islam stands out for having brought modern architecture to Bangladesh. As Senior Architect to the Government of East Pakistan (1958–64) he seems to have played a key role in having Louis Kahn invited to design the government center in Dhaka, a project with which Kahn would be deeply involved from 1965 until his death in 1974. After opening his own office in the mid-60s, Islam collaborated with the American architect Stanley Tigerman on the design of five polytechnic institutes built in Bangladesh between 1966 and 1978, for which they devised an abstract Neo-Kahnian, quasi-abstract typology in monolithic brick construction comprising a series of traditional masonry elements such as solid and hollow walls, corner buttresses, piers and column grids permutated in relation to a set of different geometrical formations among them a square, a lozenge, a cruciform and a swastika (Fig. 123). Such a lexicon combined with flat piers and repetitive castellations was employed by Islam in all his subsequent work including the Jahangirnagar University, Savar (1967–70), the Limestone Mining Housing, Joypurhat (1978–) and the National Library in Dhaka (1978–79).

One of the most innovative neo-Kahnian works to be realized in the Americas outside of the States was Moshe Safdie's Habitat built in Montreal for Expo'67 (Fig. 124). This remarkable housing complex once again synthesized concepts drawn from both Le Corbusier and Kahn, Safdie having worked briefly for Kahn after graduating from McGill University. Otherwise derived

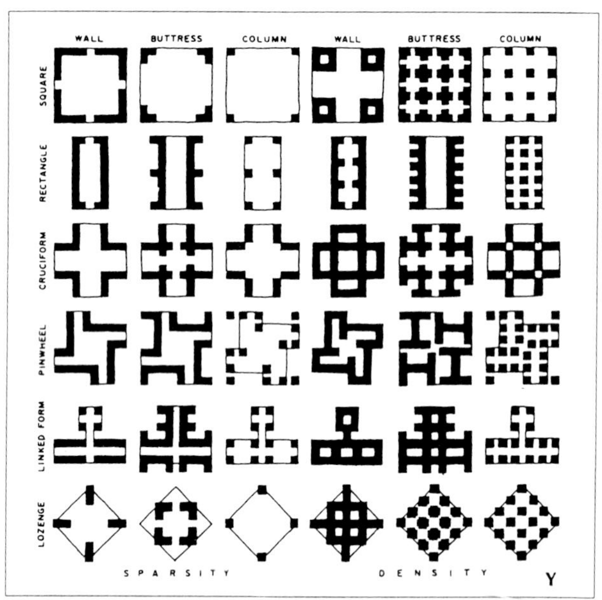

Fig. 123 Muzharul Islam and Stanley Tigerman, Tectonic/Geometric Type-forms for Bangladesh. 1970.

Fig. 124 Moshe Safdie, Habitat Expo '67, Montreal, Canada. 1967.

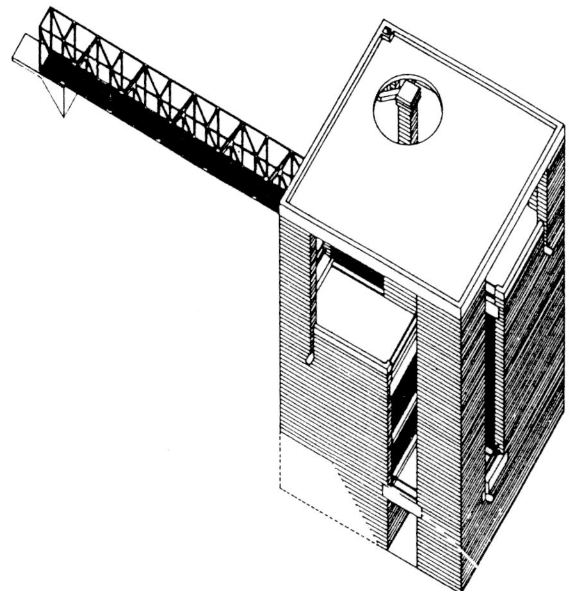

Fig. 125 Mario Botta, House in Riva San Vitale, Ticino, Switzerland. 1973. Axonometric.

from the *jardins suspendus* of Le Corbusier's Immeubles Villas proposal of 1922, this ten-story residential lattice-like structure consisted of 158 interlocking, stepped apartments stacked on top of a typically Kahnian tetrahedral space-frame, executed in reinforced concrete to the designs of Kahn's engineer Auguste Kommendant. In this complex the roofs of the lower apartments served as the garden terraces for the ones stacked above. Significantly enough this was one of the first apartment buildings in the world to be built entirely of prefabricated concrete boxes lifted into position by tower crane. As it happens, Safdie was far from being the only Western architect who would be mutually influenced by both Kahn and Le Corbusier. The Ticinese architects Aurelio Galfetti and Mario Botta were also variously influenced by Kahn as is evident from their earliest houses built respectively in Bellinzona and Riva San Vitale in 1961 and 1973 (Fig. 125).

To this neo-Kahnian genealogy we must now also add the late 70s work of the German rationalists Oswald Mathias Ungers and Josef Paul Kleihues who respectively moved away from their earlier Brutalist and Organic beginnings (see Ungers' own brickfaced house in Cologne of the mid-50s and Kleihues's initial apprenticeship with Scharoun) to follow a particular Neo-Kahnian line as this had been evolved in the mid-60s by the Italian architects Aldo Rossi and Giorgio Grassi. While one can hardly call this latter day German work truly Kahnian, it is certainly grounded in a similar formal all but schematic rigor as one may judge from Kleihues's first canonical work, his municipal street clearing garage building for Berlin of 1980 and from Ungers' "metaphysical" high rise office building that he realized for the Frankfurtmesse in 1984. These works were as much a categorical departure from Neo-Functionalist work of Ungers' professor at Karlsruhe, Egon Eiermann (see Eiermann's Neckermann complex realized outside Frankfurt in 1956) as they were the total antithesis of the postwar *Scharounschule* of Benisch et al.

Finally one must mention in the light of Kahn and the Italian Tendenza, the parallel structuralist thinking of the Dutch architect Aldo Van Eyck, who was equally committed to the idea of a "timeless", transhistorical architecture, that initially was also predicated on the reiteration of pavilionated square models as we find this in Van Eyck's orphanage erected on the outskirts of Amsterdam in the late 50s, with which he first postulated his quasiethnographic ideal of "labyrinthine clarity".

3.5 Critical Regionalism

First formulated as a category in 1981 by Alex Tzonis and Liane Lefaivre in their seminal essay of that year treating with the works of the Greek architects Dimitris and Susana Antonakakis (Atelier 66), the generic concept of Critical Regionalism, was certainly not seen as simulating some form of autochthonous vernacular, as in the case of earlier more demagogic regional modes, such as that sponsored by the Third Reich between 1933 and 1945, under the aegis of the term *Heimatstil*. Among the factors contributing more or less spontaneously to some form of Critical Regionalism is not only a measure of prosperity but also an aspiration to some form of socio-economic and political independence. The idea of Critical Regionalism is a paradoxical proposition not only because of the fundamental antithesis obtaining between rooted culture and universal civilization but also because, as Harwell Hamilton Harris implies in the citation at the head of this section, all cultures depend for their intrinsic development on a certain cross-fertilization with other cultures. Thus Harris would posit in the mid 50s the notion of a "liberative regionalism" as this pertained to the building culture of Southern California at that moment. Harris found it to be a culture that was particularly in tune with emerging thought of the time. As he put it at the time, "we call such a manifestation regional because it has not yet emerged elsewhere."

The modern Catalan regionalist ethos which first emerged with the foundation of Grup R in Barcelona in 1952 was even more of a self-conscious, anti-centrist formation. Led by J. M. Sostres and Oriol Bohigas, it found itself suspended between a desire to return to the pre-war Rationalist, anti-Fascist values of GATEPAC (the pre-war Spanish wing of CIAM) and a need to evolve a realistic regional expression accessible to the populace in Catalonia as it gradually came to terms with a more liberated political situation. This dilemma was first touched on by Bohigas in his essay, "Possibilities for a Barcelona Architecture", published in 1951. The various impulses that made up the beginnings of this movement tend to confirm the unavoidably hybrid nature of any critical local culture. Thus in the first place, there was the Catalan brick tradition to be combined with the influence of Neutra and Neo-Plasticism – the latter indubitably revived as a result of Bruno Zevi's study *La Poetica dell'architettura neoplastica* published in 1953. There followed the influential Neo-Realist architecture of the Italian architect Ignazio Gardella, who employed traditional shutters, narrow windows and wide overhanging eaves in his Casa Borsalino built in Alessandria, Italy in the same year. To this must be added, particularly for the practice of Mackay, Bohigas and Martorell, the distant influence of British New Brutalism.

The career of the Barcelona architect J. A. Coderch was quintessentially regionalist inasmuch as it oscillated between the Mediterraneanized brick "vernacular" of his eight-story ISM apartment block built in Barcelona in the Paseo Nacional in 1951 (articulated like Gardella's Casa Borsalino with full-height shutters and thin overhanging cornices) (Fig. 126) and the avant-gardist, Neo-plastic composition of his Casa Catasús completed at Sitges in 1956 (Figs. 127 & 128).

Equally Italian in its affinities but referential to Terragni's Casa del Fascio was Alejandro de la Sota's Governor's Palace, completed in Tarragona in 1957 (Fig. 129). The appeal of de la Sota's approach arose in large part from the flexibility of his method, that is to say from his evident capacity for spatial variation within the rule and for the laconic articulation of constructional form. It is a measure of de la Sota's sophistication that he would render the Governor's Palace as

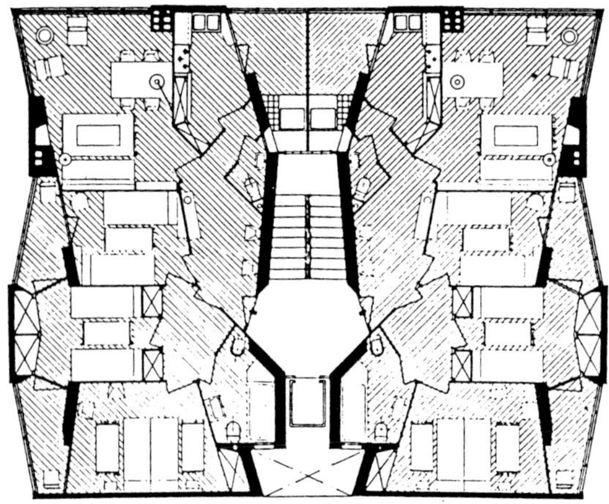

Fig. 126 J.A. Coderch, ISM Apartments, Barcelona, Spain, 1953. Plan.

Fig. 127 J.A Coderch, Casa Catasús, Sitges, Barcelona. Spain 1956.

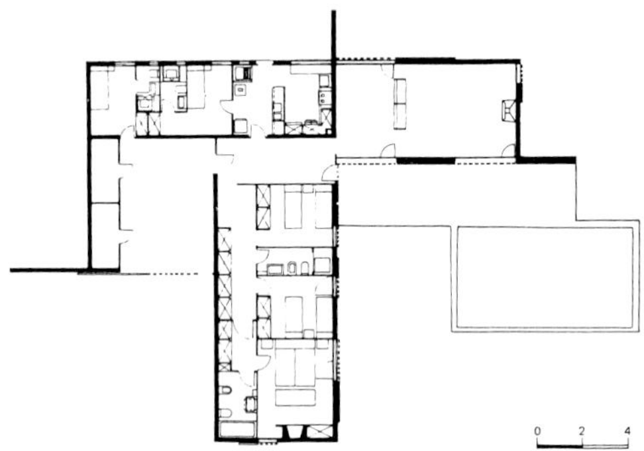

Fig. 128 J.A Coderch, Casa Catasús, Sitges, Barcelona. 1956. Plan.

a symbolic point of transition in terms of both politics and architecture. For him the mid 50s epitomized a moment when the traditional monumentality of stone, so favored by authority, could be rendered as a dynamic screen-like wall, similar in its effect to the paradoxical weightless masonry that Mies had employed in the Barcelona Pavilion in 1929. After the realization of his Neo-Constructivist Colegio Maravillas in Madrid (1961–62) de la Sota's self-effacing but dynamic architecture was widely received as a kind of normative method in Spain. Prominent among his subsequent followers we many count the partnership of Victor López Cotelo and Carlos Puente, particularly for their Zaragoza library of 1990. The influence of de la Sota is also evident in the work of the Catalan architects Esteve Bonell and Francese Rius, above all perhaps in their velodrome built in the Val d'Hebron, near Barcelona in 1984 and in their basketball arena at Badalona of 1991 (Fig. 130).

Harris's concept of "liberative regionalism" evidently manifested itself in various ways in the 50s and 60s not only in Southern California and Spain but throughout the world under different

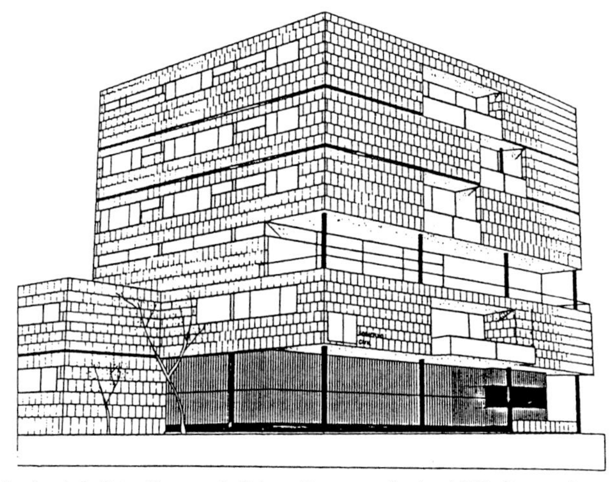

Fig. 129 Alejandro de la Sota, Governor's Palace, Tarragona, Spain. 1957. Perspective.

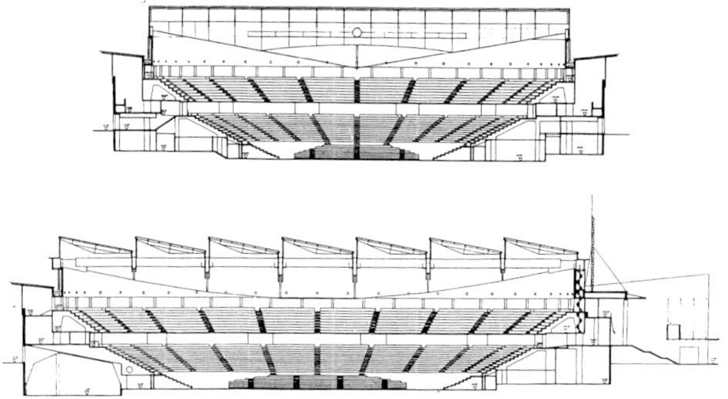

Fig. 130 Bonell and Rius, Badalona, Basketball Arena. Section.

circumstances. One has in mind for instance the roles played by locally committed architects in Finland, Sweden, Spain, Greece and Turkey, figures who would arrive at their maturity through subtle re-interpretations of the native tradition. One may even claim Gunnar Asplund's Nordic Classic Stockholm Public Library of 1928 (Fig. 131) as a regional manifestation and along with this Alvar Aalto's Viipuri Library of 1935 not to mention Aalto's Neo-National Romantic manner of the years 1934–79. By a similar token Greece and Turkey in the 50s and 60s saw other kinds of regionally inflected modern works such as the distinctly different topographic sensibilities cultivated by Dimitri Pikionis and Aris Konstantinidis, I have in mind Pikionis's landscape on the

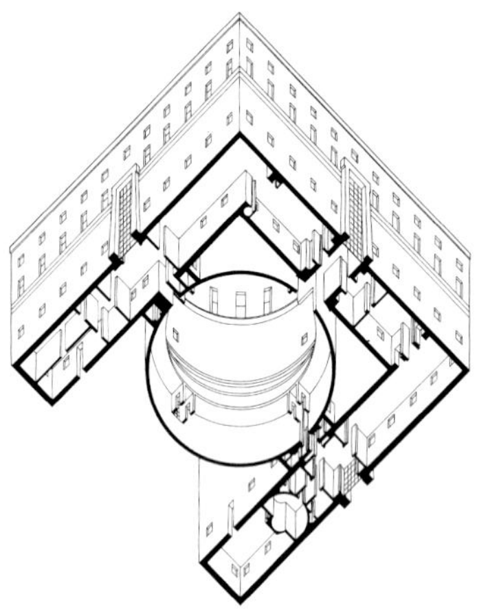

Fig. 131 Gunnar Asplund, Stockholm Public Library, Stockholm, Sweden. 1928. Axonometric.

Fig. 132 Dimitri Pikionis, Philopapou Hill, Athens, Greece. 1959. Site plan.

Fig. 133 Aris Konstantinidis, Kalambaka Hotel, Meteora, Greece 1960.

Philopapou Hill, in Athens of 1959 (Fig. 132) and Konstantindis's pitch-roofed, Kalambaka Hotel built in Meteora in 1960 (Fig. 133) which was one of a series of hotels designed for the Xenia organization in which he tried to inflect his structural rationalist approach so as to accord with the terrain in which it was situated. A similar tectonic / topographic approach will be pursued by the

Fig. 134 Sedad Hakim Eldem, Social Security Building, Zeyrek, Istanbul. 1964. Elevation in context.

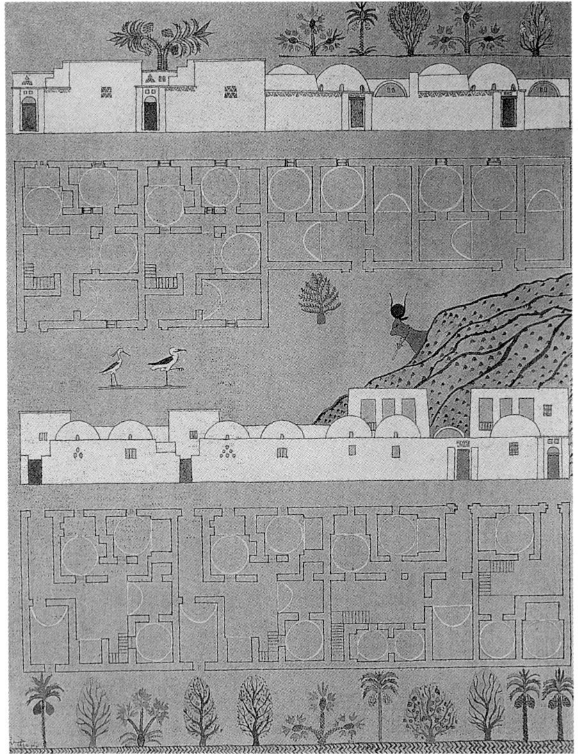

Fig. 135 Hassan Fathy, New-Gourna, Egypt, 1948. Plan.

Turkish architect Sedad Hakim Eldem, divided throughout his career between a drive to re-vitalize native domestic culture in modern terms and a more universal commitment to an expressive tectonic form, the two countervailing impulses reaching a compelling synthesis in his Social Security building realized in Zeyrek, Istanbul in 1964 (Fig. 134).

On occasion a regionally inflected modern architectural culture has stemmed from the use of a single material as in the case of the Egyptian architect Hassan Fathy who, in his life-long pursuit of low-cost, low-rise housing, would return to the archaic Middle Eastern technique of building exclusively out of sun-dried brick (Fig. 135). A comparable mono-material expression may be found in certain parts of Latin America above all perhaps in the normative high quality brick architecture realized by Togo Díaz for the city of Córdoba in Argentina or the folded shell constructions in reinforced brickwork built by the brilliant Uruguyan engineer Eladio Dieste. Last but not least, as far as the Americas are concerned, one may cite the exemplary Casa de Huéspedes realized by the Colombian architect Rogelio Salmona in the coastal city of Cartagena in 1985. (Fig. 136)

Fig. 136 Rogelio Salmona, Casa de Huespedes, San Felipe Fortress, Cartagena, Colombia. 1985.

Part 4:

Production, Place and Reality 1927–1990

Building, which in the last analysis is a material struggle against the destructive forces of nature, obliges us to face the consequences of advances in science and the discoveries and inventions of technology, in order to identify with every available aid and technique, the new laws of harmony between mass and space. As the conditions were very different from those applying to a house built by craftsmen and it was therefore impossible to predict the effect of the new, previously unknown cause, or even to realize the new laws of building within the canon of classical ornamentation, only resolute decisions, based firmly on materials, methods and technology, could establish the true way ahead.
Konrad Wachsmann, *The Turning Point of Building, 1961* [28]

What the word for space, *Raum*, designates is said by its ancient meaning. *Raum* means a place cleared or freed for settlement and lodging. A space is something that has been made room for, something that is cleared and free, namely within a boundary, Greek *peras*. A boundary is not that at which something stops but, as the Greeks recognized, the boundary is that from which it begins presencing. That is why the concept is that of *horismos*, that is, the horizon, the boundary. That for which room is made is always granted and hence is joined, that is gathered, by virtue of a location, that is by such a thing as a bridge. *Accordingly spaces receive their being from locations and not from "space".*
Martin Heidegger, *Building, Dwelling and Thinking*, 1954 [29]

4.1 The Ascendancy of the Product-Form

I have expounded at length on the work and influence of Kahn because, amongst other things, his architecture turns on the opposition between the *process* of modernization and the inherently *static* character of architecture. While Kahn initially embraced space-frame construction for its potential to engender a new building culture, as this could be derived from a totally unprecedented geometry, he seems to have soon realized that the representational task of architecture could not be readily achieved through dematerialized form. At the same time it is clear that Kahn was also attracted to the prospect of being able to construct through the assembly of prefabricated components. He soon became aware however that the complexity of the average institution, the durability of its fabric, its representational character and above all its foundation in the ground, mutually conspired to render civic buildings inimicable to the consistent application of rationalized light-weight building technique; that a certain *gravitas*, as it were, was essential to the constitution of monumental form.

Despite such concerns, it becomes increasingly clear that, with the decline of craft, quality as well as quantity may only be readily attained through the application of rationalized, more or less Taylorized methods. Early indications as to what the industrialization of building might entail first surfaced in Germany in the second half of the 20s; in Walter Gropius' Törten Siedlung Dessau and in Ernst May's Praunheim and Hohenblick housing estates in Frankfurt, all three schemes being constructed out of heavyweight, prefabricated concrete elements hoisted into position by tower cranes running on rails. This literal on-line production was subsequently elaborated into a hypothetical system for the continuous "extrusion" of dwellings by Albert Speer in 1943, in anticipation of the reconstruction of Europe that, it was supposed, would follow the triumph of the Third Reich at the end of the war. While this on-line method was not destined to be generally applied at the time, it nonetheless anticipated the heavyweight pre-cast concrete, systems that were extensively deployed in France and Scandinavia, as well as in the Soviet Union and its satellites after the war, especially during the 20-year period of post-war reconstruction.

One should note the wholesale prefabrication of modern housing units in Europe after 1945 necessitated the intervention of the state, irrespective of whether this was state Socialism in the East or the neo-capitalist welfare state in the West, for only the nation-state had the capacity to order sufficient units to justify the investment in Taylorized prefabricated systems. The fact that the dwellings produced by such systems were limited in terms of their spatial flexibility and technical refinement testifies to one of the fundamental differences between the mass production of automobiles and the application of a similar procedure to the production of dwelling units. Moreover it has since become clear that the large amounts of capital necessary for the refinement of the automobile, from prototype to production stage, only becomes readily available because of the guaranteed marketability of the car as indispensable means of private transport. On the other hand unlike the automobile, that amortizes rapidly, the residential fabric, despite its seeming repetition, has a non-consumerist character. It has to be adapted to all sorts of varied site conditions that impose constraints on its repeatability. The car is a discrete object and a consumer good by definition, which the dwelling evidently is not. Hence dwelling is not susceptible to the benefits of industrial production on anything like the same scale. We should also note that the mass ownership of the automobile in the United States, assured after 1945 by massive government subsidies for the inter-state freeway system, led not only to the proliferation of the suburban megalopolis, but also to the economic decline and abandonment of the American provincial city, accompanied by the contrived dissolution of the American transcontinental railway system.

Prior to this historical denouement, the potential for the rationalized production of one-off light-weight metal structures comes to the fore in the 30s and 40s, above all in Jean Prouvé's all-metal modular panel system applied to the Maison du Peuple, Clichy, Paris, realized in 1938 and in Richard Buckminster Fuller's pressed-metal, circular Wichita House, produced as a prototype on the assembly line of the Beech Aircraft Company in 1946. However, unlike the work of Prouvé, Buckminster Fuller's experimental structures have a marked *acultural* character, from his Dymaxion House of 1927 (Fig.137) to his pressed metal automobile and bathroom designs of 1933 and 1938, as well as his invention of the geodesic dome in 1949 which was his only device to obtain wide application, first in his 384-ft. diameter Union Tank Car Dome, built at Baton Rouge, Louisiana (1959) and then in the US Marine portable storage domes of 1962 (Fig.138) and a similar multiple deployment for the early warning DEW line Radomes erected in the Arctic throughout the period of the Cold War.

Despite the fact that Fuller's Dymaxion inventions (the neologism signifying "maximum advantage gain for minimum energy input") were to prove inapplicable to society at large except in respect of its certain survival situations, he nonetheless exercised considerable influence on the emergence of the British Hi-Tech movement which, anticipated in Cedric Price's Fun Palace of

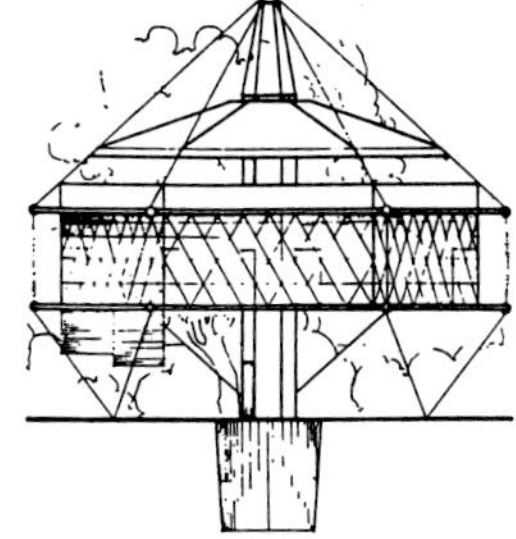

Fig. 137 Richard Buckminster Fuller, Dymaxion House. 1927. Elevation.

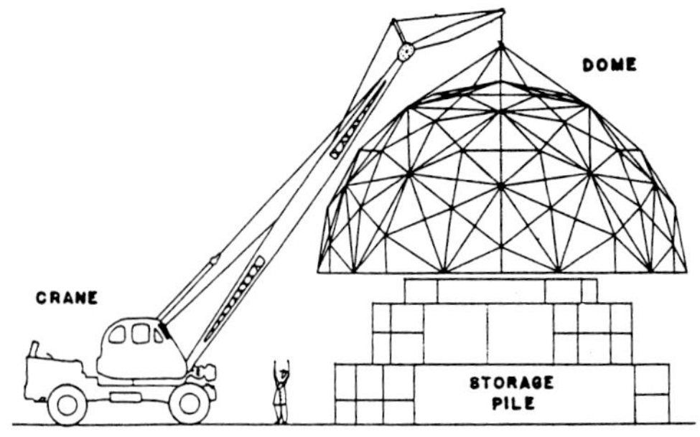

Fig. 138 Richard Buckminster Fuller, US Marine Dome. 1962. Elevation.

1961, came to the fore with the technological *tour de force* of the Centre Pompidou built in Paris to the designs of the Anglo-Italian partnership of Richard Rogers and Renzo Piano in 1977 (Fig. 139).

Subject to the influence of Fuller but not limited by Fuller's preoccupation with tetrahedral geometry, the British "hi-tech" architect Norman Foster developed Fuller's Dymaxion precept into a well-serviced envelope, at times sustained by space-frame technology as in his Climatroffice proposal of 1971, designed in collaboration with Fuller himself (Fig. 140). This well serviced, open plan structure will be subsequently re-worked as a curtain-walled, reinforced concrete building in the Willis Faber & Dumas insurance offices realized by Foster Associates in Ipswich in 1975 (Figs. 141 & 142). Structured about a concrete column and waffle floor slab, this building was enclosed on its undulating perimeter by a skin of frameless plate glass hung from the cornice of its roof slab. The resulting dematerialized form, clad throughout in tinted glass, recalled Mies van der Rohe's glass skyscrapers of the early 20s and this minimalist "almost nothing" will be returned to in one

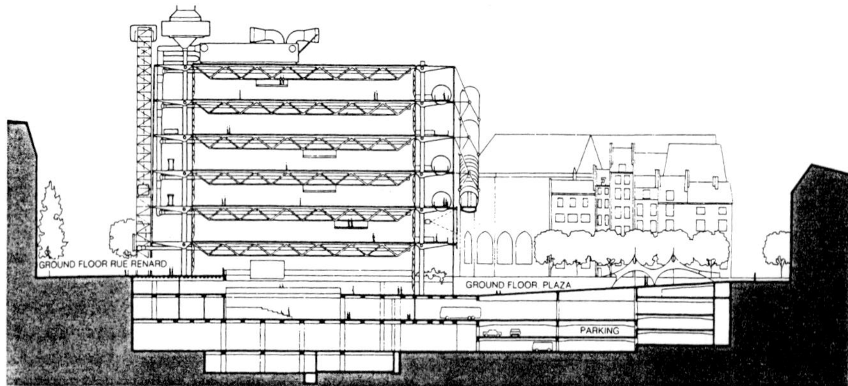

Fig. 139 Richard Rogers and Renzo Piano, Centre Pompidou, Paris, France. 1977. Section.

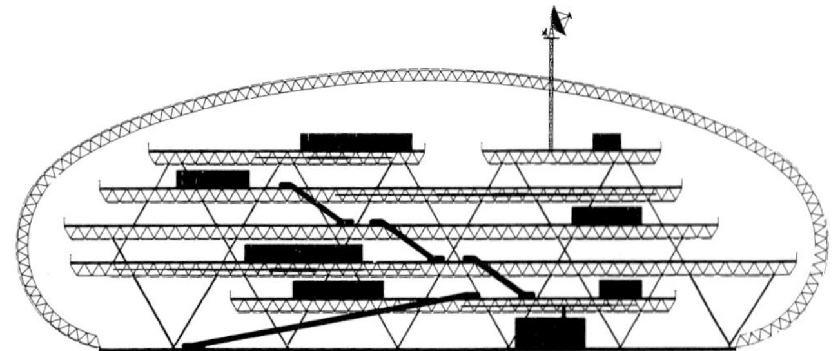

Fig. 140 Norman Foster and R. Buckminster Fuller, Climatroffice. 1971.

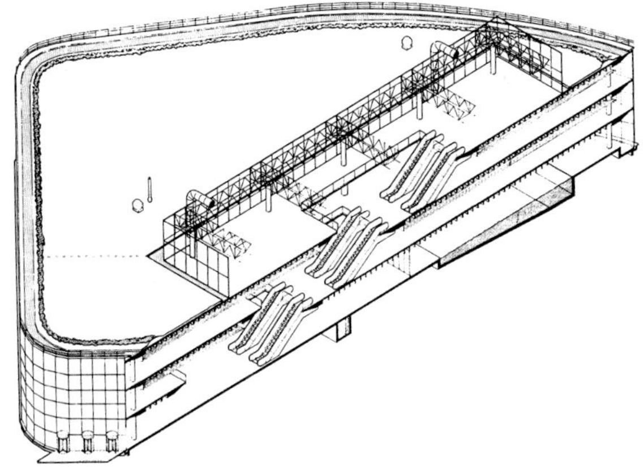

Fig. 141 Foster Associates, Willis Faber & Dumas Offices, Ipswich, England. 1975. Axonometric.

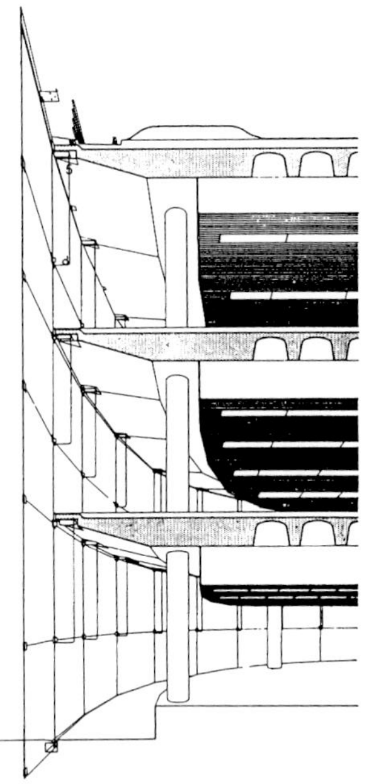

Fig. 142 Foster Associates, Willis Faber & Dumas Offices, Ipswich, England. 1975. Section through perimeter.

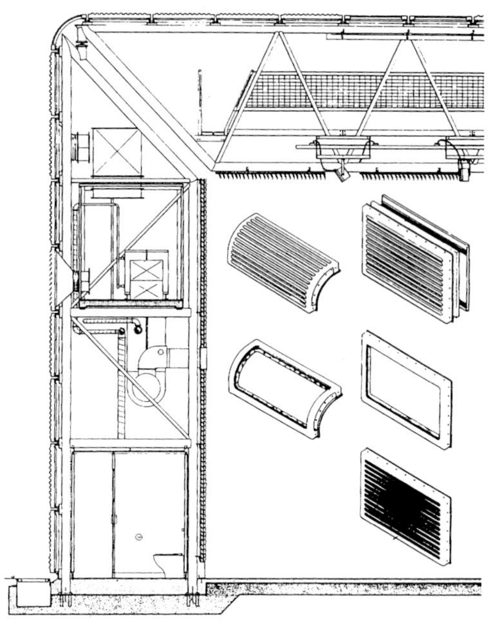

Fig. 143 Foster Associates, Sainsbury Centre for Visual Arts, University of East Anglia, Norwich, England. 1975. Section.

Foster building after another from the Sainsbury Centre for Visual Arts at the University of East Anglia, Norwich (1975) (Fig. 143) to the Hong Kong and Shanghai Bank, Hong Kong (1986) (Figs. 144, 145 & 146), and the new Hong Kong Air Terminal (1998). In the first and last of these works the basic structure is within and the waterproof membrane without, while in the 42-story bank building the verticality of the structure is modulated by suspending the building within a gigantic tubular steel skeleton, thereby breaking down the scale of the megastructure into five units (Fig. 144).

An alternative approah to rationalized production in steel, was the dry assembly of light-weight,

Fig. 144 Foster Associates, Hong Kong & Shanghai Bank, Hong Kong, China. 1986.

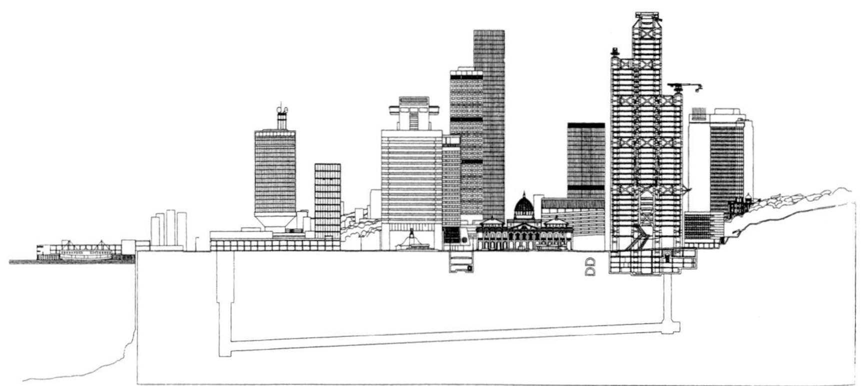

Fig. 145 Foster Associates, Hong Kong & Shanghai Bank, Hong Kong, China. 1986. Site section.

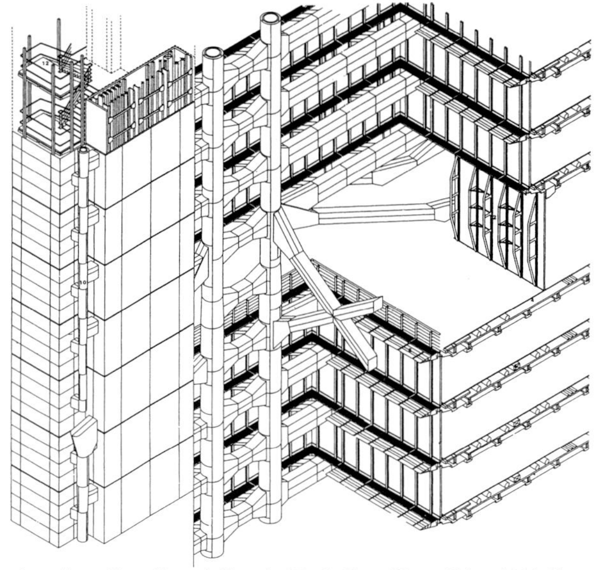

Fig. 146 Foster Associates, Hong Kong & Shanghai Bank, Hong Kong, China. 1986. Cut away axonometric. Construction details.

pre-cast concrete components, that Kahn developed with his engineer Auguste Kommendant. This would be brought to a particular level of refinement in Heman Hertzberger's Central Beheer insurance company office building, completed at Apeldoorn in Holland in 1974 (Figs. 147 & 148). Here apart from the use of a pre-cast, reinforced concrete frame, with cantilevered veirendeel trusses supporting the floor plates, Hertzberger opted for a "labyrinthic" articulation of the or-

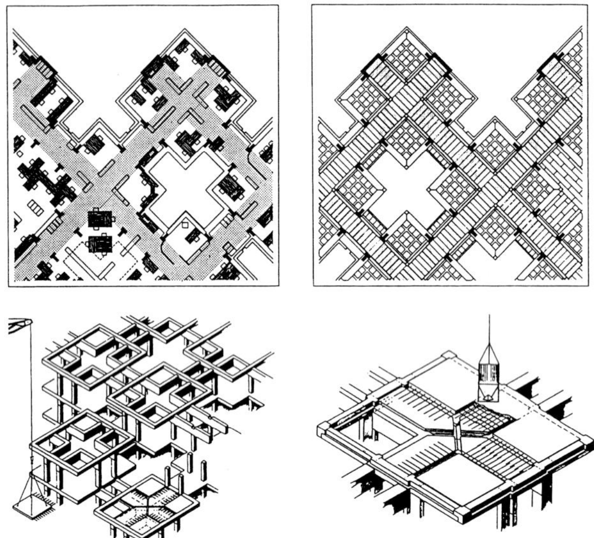

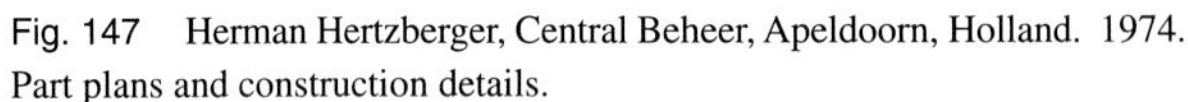

Fig. 147 Herman Hertzberger, Central Beheer, Apeldoorn, Holland. 1974. Part plans and construction details.

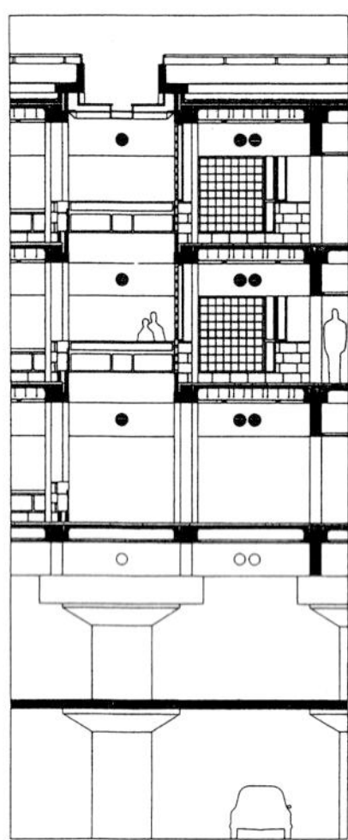

Fig. 148 Herman Hertzberger, Central Beheer, Apeldoorn, Holland. 1974. Section.

thogonal volume in order to combine the introspective, open-office floor space of Wright's Larkin Building of 1906 with the cellular, "casbah" character such as we find in Safdie's Habitat of 1967. Through the proliferation of similar labyrinthine complexes, as these had been first advocated by Aldo Van Eyck in the mid-50s, Hertzberger sought to overcome the reductive functionalism of the modern movement by providing polyvalent spaces of which he wrote in 1963:

> Instead of this collective interpretation of individual living patterns it is necessary to create prototypes which allow for individual interpretations of the collective pattern, i. e. we must make the houses uniform in a special way; in such a way that each individual is able to effect in it his or her own interpretation of the collective pattern.
>
> Any uniform dwellings, therefore must in the same period of time, must be capable of accommodating alternating meanings. This analogy makes it clear that place and time can be eliminated and substituted by a single, focal point of departure, i. e. that meanings are capable of changing their abode. [30]

Thus while Centraal Beheer and Willis Faber & Dumas were both built for insurance companies in provincial towns, no two structures ostensibly dedicated to the same end could have been more different, not only in terms of their tectonic expression as this was inseparable from their mode of production, but also in terms of their different interpretations of the principle of open office landscape (*Burolandschaft*). Such differences were also reflected in the social implications of their spatial organization, with Central Beheer tending towards an anarchic appropriation of space, mixing work and relaxation indiscriminately, and Willis Faber favoring a more controlled attitude in which the Panoptic organization of the office space would be compensated for by the provision of a greensward / restaurant on the roof and a swimming pool on the ground floor.

Apart from the technical elegance of his production, some of it being derived from the aerospace industry, Foster has been at his most critical of late in the micro-climatic treatment of his internal space, as we may find in the suspended winter gardens of his 55-story Commerzbank, completed in Frankfurt in 1997 (Figs. 149 & 150). Of this Andrea Compagno has written:

> In colder periods of the year the glazing of the winter garden remains closed, so that air in the winter garden can warm up, as in a greenhouse, and act as a climate buffer zone. When the windows in the winter garden are opened on warmer days the outer air flows

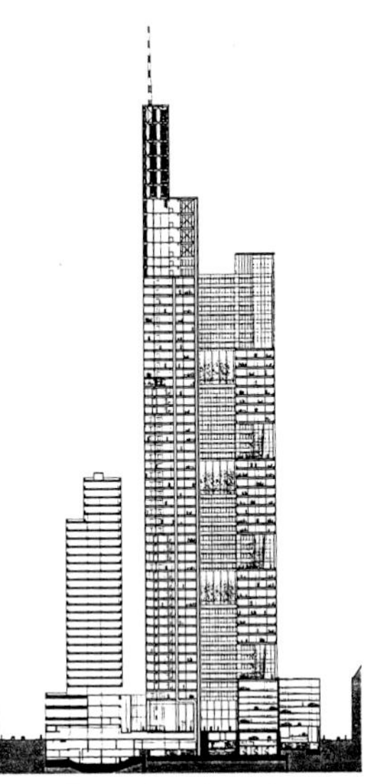

Fig. 149 Foster Associates, Commerzbank, Frankfurt, Germany. 1997. Section.

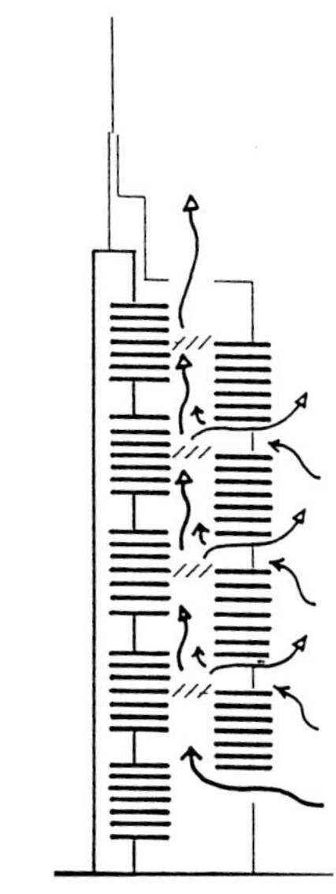

Fig. 150 Foster Associates, Commerzbank, Frankfurt, Germany. 1997. Section showing natural ventilation of the structure.

> in and rises or falls in the multi-storey atrium, depending on the temperature and pressure conditions at the time, and exits at the next winter garden. Thanks to this flow of fresh air the people working in the inner zones can naturally ventilate their office space by opening the windows. [31]

A similar attempt to modulate the internal climate of a building by natural means in evident in Renzo Piano's work whose Hi-Tech approach is otherwise characterized by a more nuanced inflection of the *product-form* according to the institutional nature of the building and the topographical character of its site. Thus, while the design and productive method remains essentially the same, a totally different tectonic syntax and referential system is evident as one passes from Renzo Piano's San Nicola Stadium in Bari (1990) (Figs. 151 & 152) to his perimeter block housing in the rue de Meaux, Paris (1991) and his Tjibaou Cultural Center in Nouméa, New Caledonia of 1999. Where the stadium may be understood as an engineering solution, having little if any cultural connotations, this superficial impression is soon dispelled once one examines the subtlety with which the work is related to its surroundings. To this end, the placement of an elliptical concrete tribune on a part natural, part artificial earthwork establishes the structure as an object which is fully integrated into its site, both topographically and historically. At the same time the division of the elevated seating into 26 cantilevered concrete "petals", fanning out around the arena, not only facilitates social control through the subdivision of the crowd into manageable units, but also permits constant visual connection between the interior of the stadium and the surrounding countryside. The sun-shading of the arena through a continuous Teflon canopy supported on steel arms and tubular steel stays rising above the tribune testifies to Piano's mastery over different productive processes, as does his capacity to assemble the concrete "petals" out of T-shaped, segmental pre-cast beams.

A similar mastery is manifest in Piano's rue de Meaux housing, designed with his partners Noriaki Okabe and Bernard Plattner. Here the primary tectonic play lies in the terracotta cladding of the elevations which are otherwise glazed or faced in a modular grid of GRC panels. These last are fabricated as either louvered, open, or opaque units. Where they are opaque they are faced with terracotta tiles which are hung onto lugs cast into the recessed GRC paneling. The textile-like syncopation of this cladding not only provides a warm finish capable of weathering but also complements, through its iterative form, the vibrant pattern of the birch trees planted in the center of the block. Here the *product-form* seems to have been consciously considered in relation to the landscape and vice versa.

A comparable play between planting and built fabric occurs in Piano's Tjibaou, Cultural Center where the so-called "cases", referential to native Kanak hut construction, are in effect laminated

Fig. 151 Renzo Piano, San Nicola Stadium, Bari, Italy. 1987–90.

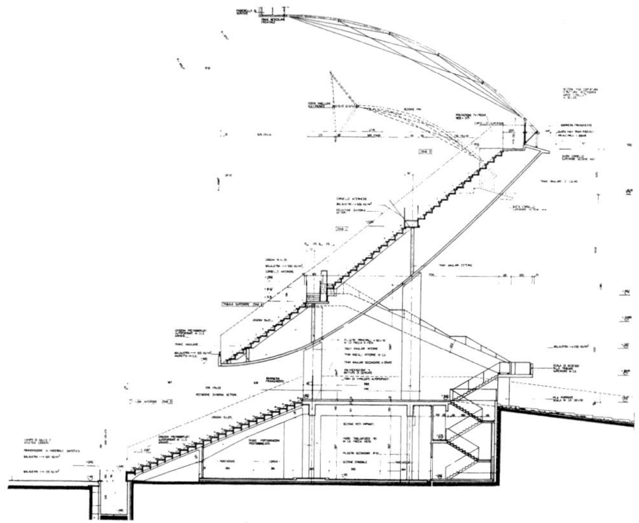

Fig. 152 Renzo Piano, San Nicola Stadium, Bari, Italy. 1987–90. Section.

timber basket-like forms reinforced with steel rods. Rising as high as 30 meters amid palm and pine plantations, these forms allude to traditional Kanak building culture without literally simulating its form (Fig. 153). Of this audacious mixing of *product-form* and *place-form* Peter Buchanan has written:

> ... the whole building was designed to be built of a mixture of specially adapted local materials and imported ones, resulting in a constructional palette much richer than those used previously by the Building Workshop. Just as the cases mixed laminated wooden

> ribs with thin slats (or even bark strip), stainless steel rods and cast-aluminum footings, so the rest of the building mixed timber posts with infills of wood boarding, glass, and pressed metal panels of various sorts... the base of the building was designed for local materials with floors of granite and retaining walls of concrete with coral aggregate. In essence, the design could be said to consist of enclosed capsules of imported high-technology materials and equipment, set on a local mineral base and wrapped around with huge husks of local vegetal matter. [32]

The slats filling the open frames of these "cases" vary in density in order to afford different degrees of sunshading, privacy and ventilation in addition to which certain louvres may be adjusted according to the direction and force of the wind, in part to induce natural ventilation and in part to protect the volume of the structure against winds of cyclonic force.

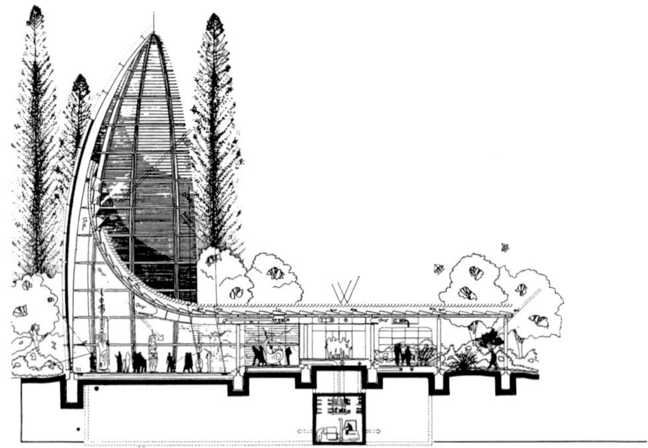

Fig. 153 Renzo Piano, Jean-Marie Tjibaou Cultural Center, Nouméa, New Caledonia, 1993. Section.

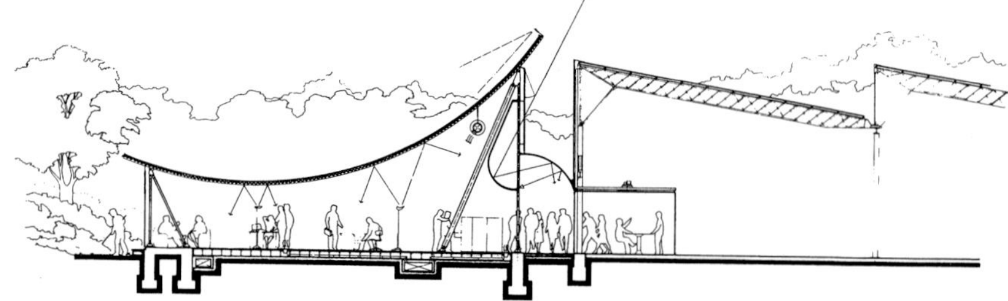

Fig. 154 Renzo Piano, Lowara Offices, Vicenza 1985. Section.

Fig. 155 Thomas Herzog, Halle 26, Hanover Trade Fair, Germany. 1996.

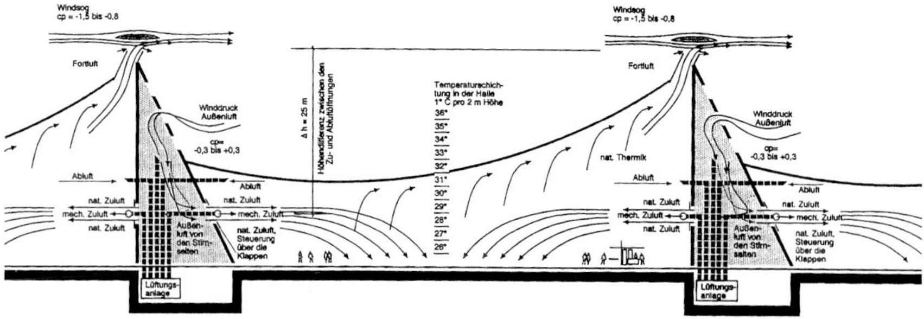

Fig. 156 Thomas Herzog, Halle 26, Hanover Trade Fair, Germany. 1996. Section.

Feedback devices and servo-mechanisms have been an essential part of Piano's practice ever since his Lowara offices, Vicenza of 1985 (Fig. 154), where a naturally ventilated catenary roof of corrugated metal could be cooled down in high summer through automatic water sprays, activated once the surface temperature of the roof exceeded a certain level. Something similar obtains in the terracotta-clad Daimler Benz Headquarters completed in Potsdamer Platz, Berlin, in 1998, for which Piano attempted to develop a double-glazed solar wall, permitting a subtle alternation between natural and artificial ventilation. A comparable homeostatic balance was sought by the German architect Thomas Herzog in his 1996 exhibition hall for the Hanover Trade Fair. (Figs.155 & 156) Here the induction of natural thermal movement facilitated the reduction of mechanical ventilation costs by half, with the cool air entering the space from ceiling ducts, thereafter to fall to the floor through convection and once again rise as it became warmer, before being exhausted through the peaks of the catenary roof covering the hall.

4.2 The Resistance of the Place-form

I have emphasized the ecological potential of the Hi-Tech approach to modern building in order to suggest how the essential climatic characteristics of a given *place* may be incorporated into the *product-form* and vice versa. That this remains an essential principle of Piano's Building Workshop was confirmed by the architect himself in 1996 when he argued that:

> There is no contradiction between technology and place, because technology is not what is was. Building technique has been transformed in the last thirty to forty years. There are completely new materials and innovative processes. Today, even the old materials may be revisited and transformed by modern techniques. Now we have composite chemical processes. If the last century was about welding, this century is about gluing. We are witness to a tremendous new potential, for the materials and the processes are changing along with the tools. When I was young, everybody told me that to make an economical structure you have to use standard pieces. This is no longer the case. In the structure of Kansai Airport every rib is different, and this is the result of a relatively simply procedure. You input the tool with a program, and the computer cuts each piece differently or stamps out any number of different pieces. If you have programmed the machine correctly, everything is perfect.
>
> The other big productive revolution is related to modern transportation. Many of my works were constructed in more than one place. For example, Kansai Airport was built on four continents. Even the small building in New Caledonia is being built in different countries. You may now fabricate a piece of building here and install it over there. However, I fail to see how this new capacity contradicts the deep feeling I have for place. Before starting a job, I spend hours in a place, just trying to capture the genius loci. There is

always a small genius, even at an abstract site like Kansai International Airport , where there was no site, no island, nothing at all. Nonetheless, we spent an afternoon in a boat with Peter Rice, thinking about metaphors, about the profile of the island and about the scale of the building. When everything is brought together, the sense of place is fundamental, but this does not contradict the impact of technology. The two factors must be brought to coexist. [33]

Fig. 157 Glen Murcutt, Marika-Alderton House, Arnhem Land, Northern Territory, Australia. 1991–94.

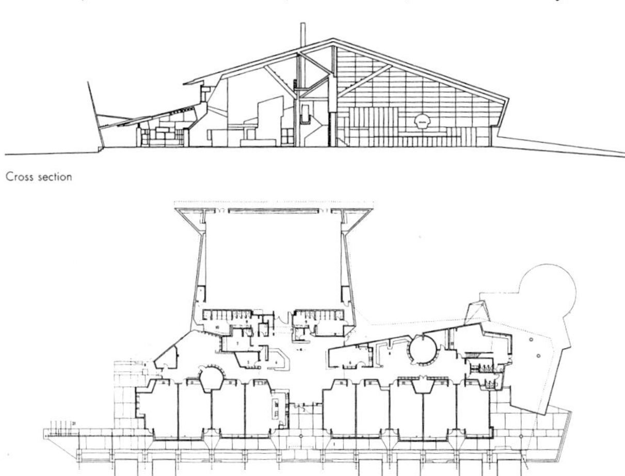

Fig. 158 John and Patricia Patkau, Seabird Island School, Agassiz, British Columbia, Canada. 1988–91. Plan and section.

However, the values of the *product-form* and the *place-form* may not always be so readily reconcilable. One has only to recognize the dystopic nature of the universal megalopolis to acknowledge how the reductive nature of consumerist production that makes itself manifest environmentally as the commercial "strip", particularly in the United States, where it certainly comes into being at the expense of the natural topography. In view of this we need to recognize the work of those late modern architects, where priority has been initially given to place-creation rather than production. One thinks of such ecologically minded architects as Glen Murcutt and Wendy Lewin of Sydney, or of John and Patricia Patkau who practice out of Vancouver. We may cite, by way of specific examples, Murcutt's Marika-Alderton House in Arnhem Land, Northern Australia of 1994 (Fig. 157) or Patkau's Seabird Island School built in Agassiz, British Columbia of 1991 (Fig. 158). In addition to these climatically responsive works, there are three other, late modern architects who have been particularly concerned with treating each commission as an occasion for creating a bounded domain, closely integrated into its context. They are Tadao Ando, Ricardo Legorreta and Alvaro Siza, respectively practicing in Japan, Mexico and Portugal. According to their location each of these architects have worked with different kinds of monolithic form, variously inflecting their designs according to the character of the place. Thus where Ando took Le Corbusier's *megaron* as his point of departure and combined it with an introspective courtyard (Fig. 159) so as to create what he termed a form of "self-enclosed modernity", Legorreta made his name with a masonry architecture, plastered and painted so as to yield a concatenation of brightly colored monolithic masses. Both men seem to have been indirectly inspired to varying degrees by Luis Barragan's introspective architecture. Thus where Legorreta would make his name with the semi-public oases of his hedonistic hotels, such as the Camino Real Hotel that he built in Ixtapa, Mexico in 1981 (Fig. 160), Ando would devote himself to the cultivation of private enclosed or semi-enclosed place-form such as we find this say in his Koshino House built in the suburbs of Ashiya, near Kobe in the same year (Figs. 161 & 162). Where Legorreta's hotel depended for its sense of security and luxury on the play of colored cubistic forms, enlivened by trees and fountains, Ando restricted himself to in-situ concrete walls, carefully detailed and proportioned so as to respond to the changing trajectory of the sun. In this context Ando appears as the more self-consciously critical architect as we may judge from his 1978 essay "The Wall as Territorial Delineation".

> The rigid-frame system is based on modernization and economic balance. It has robbed the post of its myths and the colonnade of its rhythm. Under such circumstances the wall emerges as a major theme. I am not attempting to make relative comparisons between the post and the wall or to claim that the wall is in any way superior to the post. Instead I have in mind an operation in which the wall and the post are rhetorically interrelated.
>
> The cheap sprawl and crowded conditions of the modern Japanese city reduce to a mere

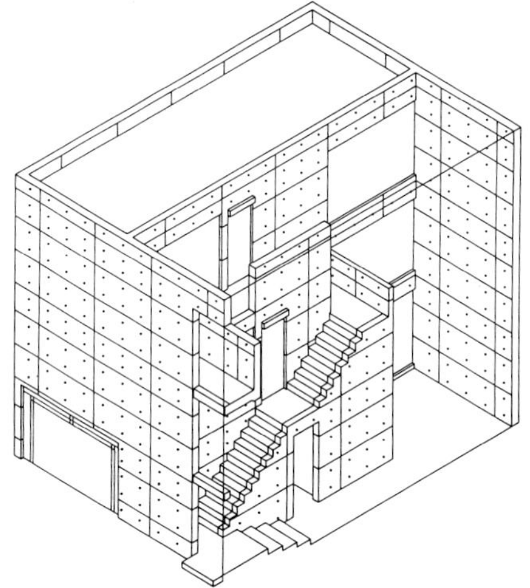

Fig. 159 Tadao Ando, House, Tokyo, Japan. 1991. Axonometric.

Fig. 160 Ricardo Legorreta, Camino Real Hotel, Ixtapa, Mexico, 1981.

dream the liberation of space by modern architectural means and the resulting close connection between interior and exterior. Today the major task is building walls that cut the interior off entirely from the exterior. In this process, the ambiguity of the wall, which is simultaneously interior and exterior is of the greatest significance. I employ the wall to delineate a space that is physically and psychologically isolated from the outside world.... I am implying that walls can be used to help break the unlimited monotony and random irrelativity of walls used in the modern urban environment. In other words, I think walls can be used to control walls.

The emergence on the scene of Robert Venturi's *Complexity and Contradiction in Architecture*, in 1966, freed the cultural level of the architectural world from its bondage to the kind of Modernism in which Le Corbusier had taken the lead. In the 1970s diversity of direction became even more apparent. No matter how brilliant and dazzling the post-Modernist cultural tendencies may be, however, unless they fundamentally evolve

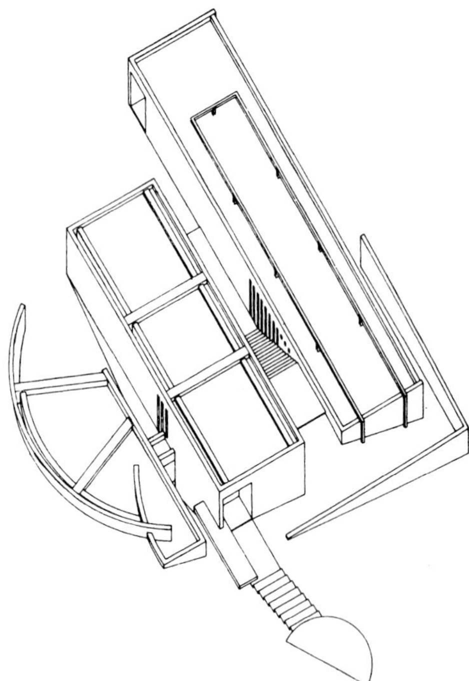

Fig. 161 Tadao Ando, Koshino House, Ashiya, Japan. 1983. Axonometric.

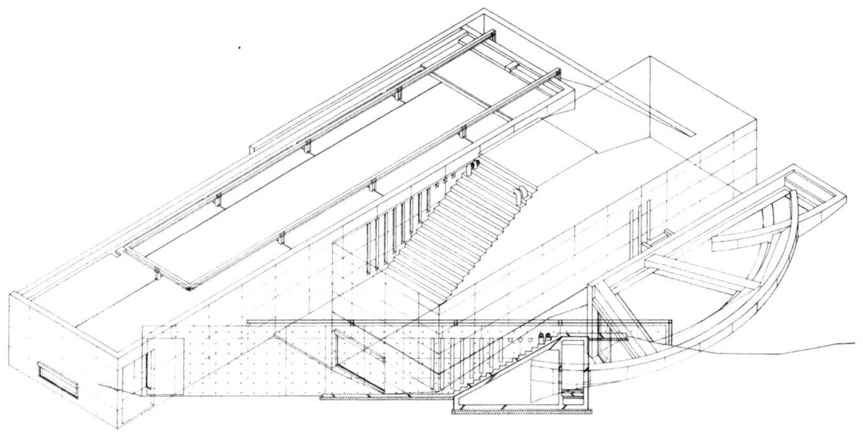

Fig. 162 Tadao Ando, Koshino House, Ashiya, Japan. 1983. Axonometric-section.

> from everyday human life, the architecture related to them cannot be expected to preserve power long as a field connected with the broader panorama of humanity. [34]

Siza's Quinta da Conceicao swimming pool completed in Matosinhos, in Portugal in 1965 (Fig. 163) is equally inscribed into its context and is possibly even more exigent with regard to the transformation of the building over time. For Siza architecture must concern itself with transforming reality rather than indulging in the gratuitous invention of aestheticized form. It is significant that among the late modern masters who have attained a certain "star" status both Ando and Siza have devoted themselves to the theme of low-rise, high-density housing. I have in mind Ando's Rokko Housing, under construction since 1978 on four self-contained sectors let into hitherto "unbuildable" sites overlooking the port of Kobe (Figs. 164 & 165), and Siza's Malagueira housing, underway on the outskirts of Evora since 1977 (Figs. 166 & 167). Here, apart from the fact that both schemes involve terrace housing, all programmatic resemblance ends since Ando's scheme is a speculative exercise in upper middle class accommodation while Siza's scheme consists of working class housing designed under the aegis of the local communist government. Despite these fundamental differences they have both been equally incrementally integrated into the topography they serve, with both architects exploiting dense, low-rise fabric as a device for restructuring the landscape.

Beyond such enclaves the received modus is quite different, particularly where the patterns of

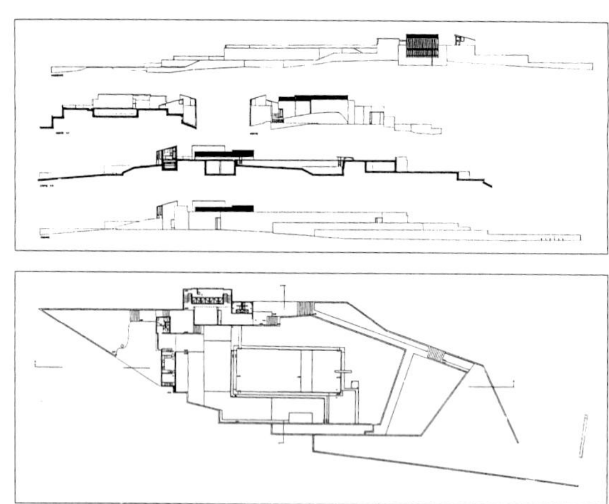

Fig. 163 Alvaro Siza, Swimming Pool, Quinta da Conceicao, Matosinhos. 1958. Plan and Sections.

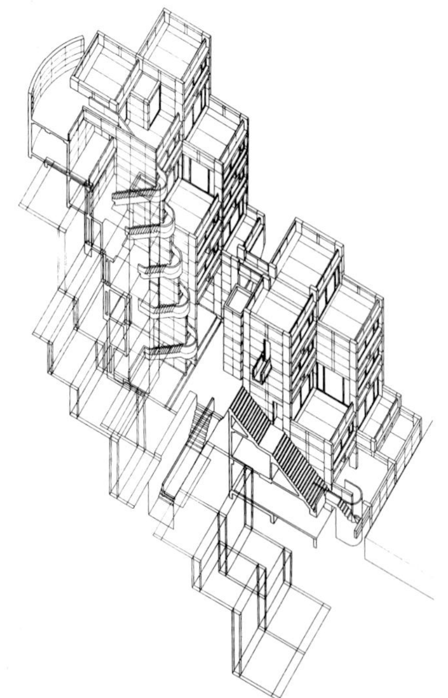

Fig. 164 Tadao Ando, Rokko Housing, Phase1, Kobe, Japan, 1978–83. Axonometric.

Fig. 165 Tadao Ando, Rokko Housing, Phase1, Kobe, Japan, 1978–83.

land settlement are determined by economic maximization. In the so-called developed world unmediated speculation spontaneously produces the all too familiar pattern of suburban sprawl, fed by the optimization of the automobile. This land settlement pattern was first fully initiated in the United States after 1945 when the building of the interstate freeway system opened up large tracts of previously inaccessible agricultural land. While the resulting dispersion of ill-related objects is more prevalent in North America than elsewhere, the current Americanization of the world in the name of *globalization* tends to proliferate similar patterns of land settlement worldwide. As Marc Augé has pointed out in his study, *Non-Places: Introduction to an Anthropology of Supermodernity*, (1992) many of the more alienating aspects of contemporary life are brought into being by the proliferation of the "non-place urban realm", to coin the American planner Melvin Webber's demagogic phase of the 1960s.

Against this catastrophic development environmental design may still project the ecological *place-form*; that is to say, a bounded domain that is inscribed into its landscape so as to create its own context and, on occasion, even to serve as a catalyst for other viable alternative patterns of settlement. I have in mind a number of exemplary projects that have succeeded in demonstrating the potential for more responsible forms of residential development; among them Kamram Diba's Shustar New Town in Iran (1972–85) and Roland Rainer's Puchenau settlement under construction on the banks of the Danube from 1960 to 1991 (Figs.168 & 169).

Fig. 166 Alvaro Siza, Malagueira Housing, Evora, Portugal, 1960–90.

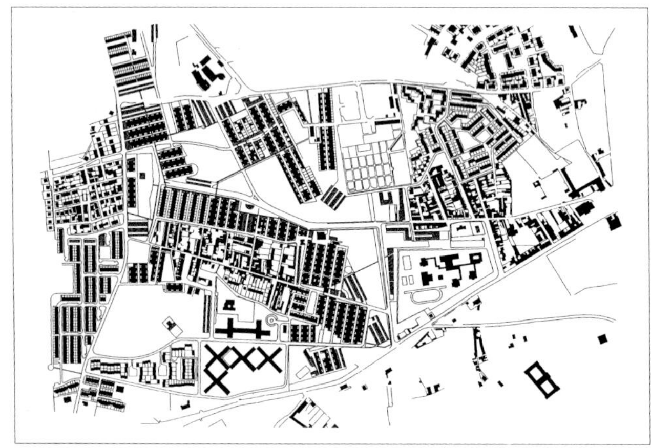

Fig. 167 Alvaro Siza, Malagueira Housing, Evora, Portugal, 1960–90. Site plan.

For Rainer it is clear that we can no longer regard the reification of the one-off object as the only viable concern for architectural culture, for we live in a world in which reparation and maintenance of the environment assumes an increasingly urgent priority and in this regard it may be claimed that the cultivation of the landscape is of greater overall consequence than the creation of architecture form. Thus as Rainer wrote of China in 1973, prior to its current modernization:

> "At such a moment [as the present] we must find interesting a world that for three or four thousand years has enabled many hundreds of millions of people to live a cultivated existence in a relatively small area – a world constructed not as a mechanism but as a garden." [35]

In the ninety years that have elapsed since the first utopian gestures of the Futurist avant-garde, radical modernism has become increasingly distanced from the life-world through the aestheticization of form, so that today little remains of the revolutionary potential of the original modern movement. From this standpoint we may even think of the modern project as the lost cause of the welfare state; one that may now only be redeemed on an ad hoc basis through the self-conscious generation of a critical practice; one which construes every commission as the occasion for the creation and maintenance of place. In the meantime the imploding urban population continues to pile-up in ever larger aggregations all over the world. In 1965 there were fewer than 400,000 squatters in Bombay in a city that then had a total population of 4.5 million. Today this population has increased to 20 million, over half of which is now made up by people living in provisional shelters of various kinds, invariably without access to either a reliable water supply or any kind of sewerage system, let alone sufficient electrical energy or an adequate pro-

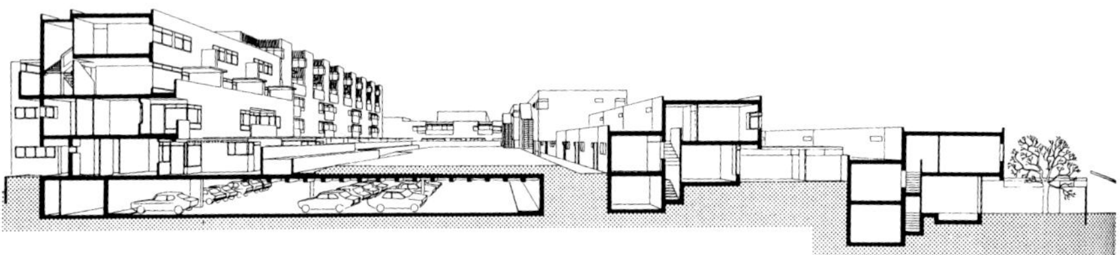

Fig. 168 Roland Rainer, Low-Rise, High-Density Housing, Puchenau, Austria, 1960–80. Section.

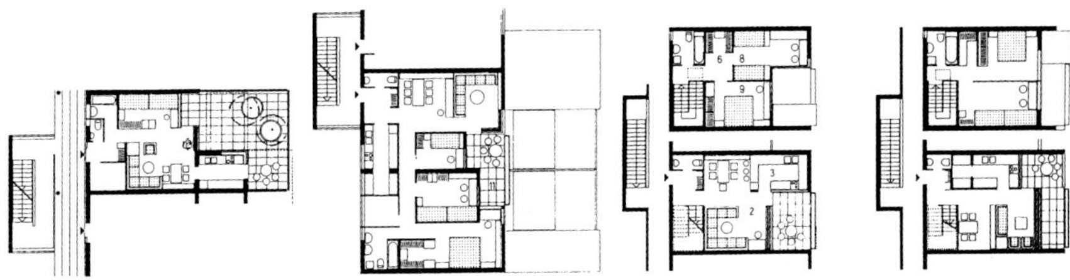

Fig. 169 Roland Rainer, Low-Rise, High-Density Housing, Puchenau, Austria, 1960–80. Typical house plans.

vision for personal hygiene and the preparation of food. It is now predicted that by the year 2015 the ten largest cities in the world will boast populations of 20 million and more. Thus it is generally expected that the world's urban population, currently set at 2.5 billion, will double over the next 25 years.

Thus modern architecture finds itself caught at the begining of the 21st century, at the threshold of the information age, in a curious double paradox for while the developed world becomes an ever more barbarous and ruined place, torn apart by multifarious forms of rapid consumerist development, a process which shows little sign of abatement, the quality of architecture worldwide, considered on an individual basis, has perhaps never been higher, thanks in large part to sophisticated forms of professional education and to the dispensations of the media which have effectively dissolved, once and for all, the former hierarchical cultural dependency between the center and the periphery. At the same time, we also know that apart from the effective loss of the traditional city (except where it still survives in old historical cores) a greater tragedy attends us beyond the confines of this urban matrix, namely our total failure as a democratic society to arrive at an accepted, normative pattern of industrial land settlement; one that would be both culturally nuanced and ecologically viable. The Chinese architect Tao Ho has recently put this dilemma in terms of an urgent need to shift from our currently non-renewable energy source of fossil fuels and nuclear power to a renewable energy base such as solar power and to a concomitant requirement to reduce our overall consumption of energy. Such a prospect surely at once presupposes not only increased if precisely moderated densities of land settlement but also surely different modes of transportation, ones which are less individualized than our current universal dependency on the automobile. The severe limits of contemporary architecture as a critical practice and the patently unfinished nature of the modern project in the Enlightenment sense, jointly point to the need for a totally new politics of the environment, which as of now shows little sign of coming into being.

Bibliography

[1] Tönnies, Ferdinand, *Community and Society*, Harper & Row, New York: 1963, p. 35
[2] Heynen, Hilde, *Architecture and Modernity*, MIT Press, Cambridge: 1999.
[3] Loos, Adolf. "Architecture." Tim and Charlotte Benton (Eds.), *Form and Function: A Source for the History of Architecture and Design 1890-1939*, pp. 41–42. Crosby, Lockwood, Staples, London: 1975.
[4] Loos, p. 45.
[5] Banham, Reyner. *Theory and Design in the First Machine Age*, p. 104. Praeger, New York: 1960.
[6] Banham, p. 129.
[7] Vladimir Tatlin, T. Shapiro, I. Meyerzon and Pavel Vinogradov, "The Work Ahead of Us." Stephen Bann (Ed.), *The Tradition of Constructivism*, p. 14. Viking Press, New York: 1975.
[8] Bann 1974, p. 146.
[9] El Lissittzky, *Russia: An Architecture for World Revolution*, MIT Press, Cambridge, 1970, p. 34.
[10] Kopp, Anatole. "Shlushali: Problemy Tipizutsii Zhil'ya R.S.F.S.R." *Town and Revolution*, Thomas E. Burton (Trans. George Brazille), p. 141. New York: 1970.
[11] Van der Rohe, Mies. "The New Era." Philip C. Johnson, *Mies van der Rohe*, p.195. Museum of Modern Art, New York, 3rd Edn., 1978.
[12] Le Corbusier. *Towards a New Architecture*, p. 187. (Trans. Frederick Etchells). Architectural Press, London: 1927.
[13] Schnaidt, Claude. *Hannes Meyer: Buildings, Projects, Writings*, Arthur Niggli Ltd, Teufen AR, 1965, p. 25.
[14] Muzio, Giovanni. "Alcuni architti d'oggi in Lombardia," Dedalo, 1931, pp. 1087–1107. Leonardo Benevolo, *History of Modern Architecture*, Vol. 2, p. 563. MIT Press, Cambridge, Mass., 1971.
[15] Gruppo 7, "11 Gruppo 7" (Trans. Ellen R. Shapiro), in *Oppositions* 6: Fall 1976, pp.90–91.
[16] Grassi, Giorgio. "Avant-Garde and Continutity." (Trans. Stephen Santavelli), *Oppositions* 21, pp. 26–27
[17] Zevi, Bruno, *Towards an Organic Architecture*, Faber & Faber, London: 1947, pp. 75, 76.

[18] Manson, Grant Carpenter, *Frank Lloyd Wright to 1910: The First Golden Age*, Reinhold Publishing Corporation, New York: 1958, p. 39.
[19] Wright, Frank Lloyd, "In the Cause of Architecture," in *Frank Lloyd Wright Collected Writings*, ed. Bruce Brook Pfeiffer, Rizzoli, New York, 1992, p. 86.
[20] Conrad, Ulrich, *Programs and Manifestoes on 20th Century Architecture*, MIT Press, Cambridge: 1970, P. 46.
[21] *Alvar Aalto*. Alec Tiranti, Lordon 1963, p. 81.
[22] Alvar Aalto "The Humanizing of Architecture" in *Alvar Aalto in His own Words*, ed. Goran Schildt, Rizzoli, New York, 1997, p. 103.
[23] Jussi Rausti, "Alvar Aalto's Urban Plans, 1940–1970" in DATUTOP 13, Tampere, 1988, p. 52.
[24] Leonardo Benevolo, *History of Modern Architecture Vol 2*, MIT, Cambridge, Routledge and Kegan Paul, London, 1971, p. 616.
[25] Harris, Hamilton Harwell, "Liberative and Restrictive Regionalism" Address given to the Northwest Chapter of the AIA in Eugene, Oregon in 1954.
[26] Ricoeur, Paul, "Universal Civilization and National Cultures" (1961), *History and Truth*, trans. Chas. A. Kelbley, Northwestern University Press, Evanston, IL, 1965, pp. 276–277.
[27] Mayekawa, K., "Thoughts on Civilization in Architecture," *AD*, May 1965, pp. 229–230.
[28] Wachsmann, Konrad, *The Turning Point of Building:Structure and Design*, Reinhold Publishing Corp., New York, 1961, p. 12.
[29] Heidegger, Martin, *Basic Writings from Being and Time*, ed. David Farrell, Harper & Row, New York, 1977, P. 54.
[30] Hertzberger, Herman, *A+U*, No. 4, April 1991, pg. 20.
[31] Compagno, Andrea, *Intelligent Glass Façades:Material Practice Design*, Birkhäuser Publishers, Basel, Boston, Berlin, 1999, pp. 143–144.
[32] Buchanan, Peter, *Renzo Piano Building Workshop-Complete Works, Vol. II*, Phaidon Press, London, 1995, p. 193.
[33] Piano Renzo, *Tecknology, Place and Architecture*, Ed., Kenneth Frampton, Rizzoli, New York, 1988, pp. 132–133.
[34] Ando, Tadao, *Tadao Ando: Buildings, Projects, Writings*, Kenneth Frampton, ed., Rizzoli, New York:1984, pp. 128, 129.
[35] Rainer, Roland, *Die Welt als Garten–China*. Akademische Druck und Verlagsanstalt, Graz, 1979, p. 7.

Acknowledgement

Photographic Credits

We gratefully acknowledge the following persons and/or institutions for the photographs in this book.

Part 1: Fig. 2, Adolf Loos, Leben und Werk, by Burchard Rukschcio and Roland Schachel, Residenz Verlag, Salzburg und Wien, 1982; Fig. 3, Henri Sauvage, ou l'exercice du renouvellement, by Jean-Baptiste Minnaert, photography by Dominique Delauney, Editions NORMA, Paris, 2002; Fig. 6, Building in the USSR 1917–1932, edited by O.A. Shvidkvsky, Praeger, New York, 1971; Fig. 11, L'Architecture Vivante, Automne & Hiver M CM XXV, ed. Albert Morancé; Fig. 12, Walter Gropius, by Sigfried Giedion, Dover Publications, Inc., New York, 1992; Fig. 14, Mies van der Rohe, by Philip C. Johnson, The Museum of Modern Art, New York, 1947; Fig. 18, Architecture of Skidmore, Owings & Merrill, 1950–1962, Praeger, New York, 1963; Fig. 30, 32, Plate 4, Architects of the Twentieth Century, text: Kenneth Frampton, Principal photography: Roberto Schezen, Harry N. Abrams, Inc., New York, 2002; Fig. 36, Lutyens, The English Architect Sir Edwin Lutyens (1869–1944), Arts Council of Great Britain, London, 1981.

Part 2: Fig. 46, Modern Architecture, 1851–1945, by Kenneth Frampton/Yukio Futagawa, Rizzoli, New York, 1981, 1983; Fig. 52, Antonin Raymond, His Work in Japan, 1920–1935, by Antonin and Noémi P. Raymond; Fig. 57, 58, Richard Neutra, by Esther McCoy, George Braziller, Inc., New York, 1960; Fig. 60, Architecture & Its Photography, by Julius Shikmaw, Taschen, Köln, 1998; Fig. 61, Space, Time and Architecture, The Growth of a New Tradition, by Sigfried Giedion, The Harvard University Press, Cambridge, 1941; Fig. 70, Erich Mendelsohn, 1887–1963, Ideen Bauten Projekte, by Sigrid Achenbach, Staatliche Museen Preussischer Kulturbesitz, Berlin, 1987; Fig. 71, Photography: Wilfried Wang; Fig. 72, The Modern Flat, by F.R.S. Yorke and Frederick Gibberd, The Architectural Press, London, 1937; Fig. 75, Behnisch & Partners, 50 Years of Architecture, text by Dominique Gauzin-Müller, photographs by Christian Kandzia, Academy Editions; Fig. 83, Architecture in the Scandinavian Countries, by M. C. Dennelly, MIT Press, 1992.

Part 3: Fig. 88, 90, Plate 1, Oscar Niemeyer, by Stamo Papdaki, George Braziller, Inc., New York, 1960; Fig. 122, Charles Correa, Thames and Hudson, Ltd., London, 1996; Fig. 124, Moshe Safide, edited by Wendy Kohn, Academy Editions; Fig. 127, J.A. Coderch de Sentimenat, 1913–1984, Editorial Gustave Gill, Sa; Fig. 133, Aris Konstantinidis, Projects and Buildings, Agra Editions, Greece, 1981; Fig. 136, Rogelio Salmona, by G. Tellez, Escala, Colombia, 1991.

Part 4: Fig. 144, Plate 2, Sir Norman Foster, by Philip Jodidio, Taschen, Köln, 1994; Fig. 151, Plate 3, Plate 9, Renzo Piano Building Workshop, Genova, Italy; Fig. 155, Plate 6, die Halle 26, ed. Thomas Herzog, Prestel, New York, 1996; Fig. 157, Plate 7, Glenn Murcutt, Buildings + Projects, 1962–2003, by François Fromonot, Thames & Hudson, London, 2003; Fig. 160, Ricardo Legorreta; Figs. 165, Plate 8, Yao Jian; Fig. 166, Plate 5, Mechthild Heuser, Zurich, Switzerland.

Index

D

E

F

G

H

I

J

K

L

M

N

O

P

Q

R

S

T

U

V

W

X

Y

Z